Choices in Health Policy

An Agenda for the European Union

Choices in Health Policy

An Agenda for the European Union

Brian Abel-Smith
Josep Figueras
Walter Holland
Martin McKee
Elias Mossialos

OFFICE FOR OFFICIAL PUBLICATIONS
OF THE EUROPEAN COMMUNITIES
Luxembourg

Dartmouth

Aldershot • Brookfield USA • Singapore • Sydney

British Library Cataloguing in Publication Data
Abel-Smith, Brian
   Choices in Health Policy: Agenda for the European Union
   I. Title
   362.1094

Library of Congress Cataloging-in-Publication Data
Choices in health policy : an agenda for the European Union / by Brian
   Abel-Smith ... [et al.].
      p.   cm.
   Includes index.
   ISBN 1-8521-755-4. – ISBN 1-85521-762-7 (pbk.)
    1. Medical policy–European Union countries. 2. Health planning-
   -European Union countries. I. Abel-Smith, Brian.
   RA395.E88C48   1995
   362.1'094–dc20   95-34904
                                                   CIP

Office for Official Publications of the European Communities
2 rue Mercier
L-2985 Luxembourg

ISBN 92-827-4573-2   Catalogue number CE-90-95-259-EN-C

Dartmouth Publishing Company Limited
Gower House
Croft Road
Aldershot
Hants GU11 3HR
England

Dartmouth Publishing Company
Old Post Road
Brookfield
Vermont 05036
USA

ISBN 1 85521 755 4 (Hbk)
     1 85521 762 7 (Pbk)

Printed in Great Britain at the University Press, Cambridge

Contents

List of Tables and Figures

Tables

Figures

Foreword

Health policy and health systems in the European Union are at a critical juncture. On the one hand there are enormous challenges to be overcome: demographic changes, increasing population mobility, growing social exclusion, costly new therapeutic techniques and rising public demands and expectations are all combining to place mounting pressure on service provision, and are doing so at a time when public spending is under tight constraints.

On the other, there are new opportunities to meet and overcome those challenges and secure substantial improvements in health. People are gaining a greater understanding of their health and there is growing interest in prevention and health promotion; clinical advances are enabling more effective and efficient forms of treatment, and information both relating to patients and about health matters in general can be circulated more widely and more rapidly. Moreover, with the coming into effect of the Treaty on European Union, there is more scope for international cooperation and for Union-wide initiatives which can provide all Member States with access to the very best expertise and greatest experience available.

Recognizing the issues that need to be faced, the Ministers for Health of the Union adopted a resolution in November 1991, on fundamental health choices. In May 1994 at the Rhodes Health Forum the Ministers for Health of the Union returned to this important topic to consider the way forward. To inform their discussions they were presented with the findings of a detailed report prepared for the European Commission by Professor Abel-Smith and his colleagues. This book is based upon that report.

It provides an authoritative survey of the main determinants of health status in the Union today, of the organization of health services and of the issues that Member States have to address in framing their policies for the future. It also identifies the areas where the European Community can play a valuable and complementary

xi

role. As such it represents an essential contribution to the continuing debate about how to achieve the best possible level of health for all citizens of the Union.

Padraig Flynn
Member of the European Commission
responsible for Employment and Social Affairs

Series Preface

European Political Economy

The first concern of the editors in establishing this series, is to encourage the study of issues of fundamental importance to the development, strength and prosperity of Europe, both East and West. Hence, we are using the term "European Political Economy" in the broadest sense, and inviting contributions from experts in many social sciences and from all European States.

With encouragement and support from the European Commission, many researchers are working together in interdisciplinary and international teams or networks to produce policy-relevant research of the highest academic standards. We are especially keen to disseminate the results of such research. It is particularly appropriate that this first volume of the series should be the product of such a team, supported by the Commission, and should concern health policy, a major policy problem across Europe.

A second of our concerns is that these research findings should be made available to the entire research community which uses English as an international language. Our aim is to produce texts which are easily comprehensible to readers of English who do not have the current cultural points of reference, or contemporary jargon of the USA, UK or any other English-speaking country.

The series editors are based in the European Institute of the London School of Economics and Political Science.

Howard Machin
Chairman of the Editorial Board

Preface

This book is based on a report to the European Commission prepared by a core research team and a team of national correspondents from all the Member States of the European Union.

We would like to thank the Directorate-General for Employment, Industrial Relations and Social Affairs (DG V) of the European Commission for providing part of the financial support for the work on which this book is based. We would especially like to thank our fellow members of the core research team. Professor Julian Le Grand took the lead in the section on inequality in health and health services and Professor Aris Sissouras contributed to the section on the utilization of health services.

We would also like to thank our two consultants – Dr Jennifer Dixon who assisted on methodologies for establishing priorities and Mr Franco Sassi who provided material from his current study on technology assessment – Dr Jean-Pierre Poullier, from OECD, who supplied unpublished data to bring some of the tables as up to date as possible and Mr Panos Kanavos, of LSE Health, for excellent research assistance.

Our greatest debt is to the 13 experts who not only provided the wealth of data from their own countries but attended two seminars at which drafts of the text were discussed at length and commented on several drafts. It may be worth mentioning that the text went through no less than 15 drafts before we, as the core research team, were satisfied with the final text set out in this volume. Last but not least, we would like to acknowledge the continuing support of Mr George Gouvras, Mr Martin Lund and Mr Bernard Merkel of DG V, each of whom attended at least one of the seminars and commented on earlier drafts. We take full responsibility for any remaining errors.

Brian Abel-Smith
Josep Figueras
Walter Holland
Martin McKee
Elias Mossialos

xv

Membership of Research Team

Chair

Professor Brian Abel-Smith, Emeritus Professor of Social Administration,
LSE Health, London School of Economics and Political Science.

Core Research Team

Dr Josep Figueras, Lecturer in Health Services Management,
London School of Hygiene and Tropical Medicine.

Professor Walter Holland, Professor of Public Health Medicine,
St Thomas's Hospital, University of London.

Professor Julian Le Grand, Richard Titmuss Professor of Health Policy,
London School of Economics and Political Science.

Dr Martin McKee, Senior Lecturer in Public Health Medicine,
London School of Hygiene and Tropical Medicine.

Dr Elias Mossialos, Senior Research Fellow, Director, LSE Health,
London School of Economics and Political Science.

Professor Aris Sissouras, Professor of Operational Research,
University of Patras.

National correspondents

Dr Jan-Maarten Boot, Senior Lecturer,
Netherlands School of Public Health, The Netherlands.

Dr Laurent Chambaud, Professor of Public Health,
Ecole Nationale de la Santé Publique, France.

Mme Marie-Christine Closon, Professor of Health Economics,
Université Catholique de Louvain, Belgium.

Dr Giovanni Fatore, Research Fellow,
Ce.R.G.A.S. Universita Commerciale Luigi Bocconi, Italy.

Dr Naomi Fulop, Senior Research Fellow in Health Policy,
London School of Hygiene and Tropical Medicine, United Kingdom.

Mr Anthony Karokis, Research Associate,
University of Patras, Greece.

Dr Allan Krasnik, Associate Professor,
University of Copenhagen, Denmark.

Dr Angel Otero, Senior Lecturer,
Centro Universitario de Estudios para la Salud Publica, Spain.

Mr Francisco Ramos, Research Fellow,
Escola Nacional de Saude Publica, Portugal.

Dr Jose Ramon Repullo, Senior Lecturer,
Escuela Nacional de Sanidad, Spain.

Dr Nils Rosdahl, Medical Officer of Health,
Medical Office of Health, City of Copenhagen, Denmark.

Mr Gisbert W. Selke, Research Fellow,
WIdO, Germany.

Dr Miriam Wiley, Head of Health Policy Research Centre,
Economic and Social Research Institute, Ireland.

Consultants

Dr Jennifer Dixon, Honorary Lecturer in Public Health Medicine,
London School of Hygiene and Tropical Medicine.

Mr Franco Sassi, Research Fellow in Health Economics,
London School of Hygiene and Tropical Medicine.

Information on Luxembourg was provided by
Dr Danielle Hansen-Koenig, Ministry of Health, Luxembourg.

Introduction

In November 1991, the Council of Ministers for Health, recognizing that it is a matter for the Member States to determine the organization and funding of their health care systems and to make fundamental choices in health policy, underlined the importance of such fundamental choices and indicated that closer cooperation and collaboration between Member States was both desirable and necessary.

This book reviews the issues underlying the need for such choices, outlines the main choices taken by the Member States, identifies the areas where cooperation and collaboration between Member States could give added value and makes recommendations for the role of Community institutions. The recommendations are focused on the two main issues facing Member States. The first is how to secure further health improvement and the second is how to secure greater efficiency in the use of health resources.

Chapter 1 sets out the main challenges to health that face Member States. It summarizes health trends, describes the extent of health and health care inequalities throughout the Union and discusses their possible causes.

Chapter 2 outlines the health care context within which choices are made by Member States. It starts with a review of the organization and financing of health care in individual Member States, then sets out the utilization of health resources and indicates the public's perception of their health services. The organization and financing of health care differs considerably between Member States as does the availability of resources, such as doctors and hospital beds, and their use by the populations they serve. There is no apparent connection between any of these and health status as judged by mortality rates.

Chapters 3 to 8 explore some of the main choices adopted by Member States, focusing on cost containment and health care reforms, health care effectiveness and technology assessment, priority setting, health promotion and prevention of disease, and the response to the health needs of migrants and ethnic minorities.

From the 1970s, the continuous rise in the cost of health care, often faster than national resources, has caused increasing concern to Member States. The pressures underlying the expansion of health care spending need not be spelt out again here. The principal factors, common to all countries are ageing populations with the growth of chronic diseases and increasing need for care, but increasingly recognized as even more important are the technological developments in health care, many of which are cost-increasing. Indeed technology is increasingly regarded as the main cause of health care cost escalation.[1,2,3] The incentives for cost-reducing technologies are too few. Also important in some countries are supplier-induced demand and rapidly rising consumer expectations.

The rise in health care costs and other changes in the face of constraints on resources leaves countries with five fundamental choices. First, they may increase the amount of resources available. Governments have the choice of raising more resources by shifting money from other areas of public sector expenditure or by raising taxes. Alternatively governments may choose to encourage individuals and families to pay for health care themselves by giving incentives for private spending. These decisions reflect political preferences and will not be discussed further in this book except to the extent that regressive or progressive approaches to funding have an impact on equity.

Second, governments may choose to control the costs of health care by controlling either the demand for services by, for example, introducing cost-sharing measures, or the supply of services by, for example, introducing budget ceilings, manpower controls or price regulation. The main response in the Member States has been an increasing series of *ad hoc* cost containment measures. Some of them have been very short term such as holding down the levels of pay or controlling prices in the health sector. Some have been likely only to achieve results on a 'once and for all' basis, such as increasing cost-sharing, reducing the scope of insurance, or limiting employment in the health sector. Others have been more fundamental such as changing the incentives facing providers by alterations in the relative value of different fees or changing the methods of remunerating health professionals. Particularly effective have been the various ways of imposing cash-limited budgets, target budgets, or quotas over the whole health sector or important parts of it. The most long-term measures have been reductions in the output of medical and dental schools and in the stock of hospital beds and the promotion of measures of prevention in the hope of reducing long-term demands for health care. Chapter 3 reviews the main measures adopted by the Member States.

Third, controls on supply of particular services may be on the basis of cost alone or may draw on evidence that many interventions are ineffective or of unknown effectiveness, or that the ratio of cost to benefit is unfavourable. Choices based on this approach seek to increase efficiency by funding only those services that are effective and of lower cost, thus releasing additional resources and containing overall expenditure. To enable Member States to make cost-effective choices more information is required on the effectiveness of health care interventions. Of particular importance is the assessment of both new and existing technologies in improving outcome and their appropriate use. While interest in technology assessment is growing, effort is widely dispersed and only to a limited extent is evidence collected on the impact of technologies on health outcome. Chapter 4 focuses on the use of outcomes information to determine what services are necessary, and describes the initial results of a survey of technology assessment activities under way in the Member States.

Fourth, several countries in the Union and elsewhere are undertaking fundamental reforms of health care to tackle rising cost through more cost-effective patterns of service provision. Several reforms seek to increase efficiency through the introduction of competition among providers and by encouraging health care purchasers to take more account of the effectiveness of the care which they buy. Examples include the introduction of provider markets in the United Kingdom and parts of Spain. There are also attempts to respond to consumer dissatisfaction by widening choice and generating competition between providers as a way of inducing providers to be more responsive to users' concerns through fear of losing patients and the money they bring with them. Chapter 3 includes a brief description of health care reforms under way in five Member States: Spain, Italy, the Netherlands, Portugal and the United Kingdom.

Fifth, as the pace of increasing demand seems to outstrip the pace of uncertain gains from efforts to increase efficiency, governments may set priorities among available interventions and client groups receiving services. One apparent consequence of cost containment measures in some Member States has been an increase in the waiting time for appointments with specialists and for admission to hospital. This is an unpopular form of rationing with risks for some that their condition will deteriorate and discomfort for many of those waiting for care. Priorities have always been set implicitly and governments may choose to continue to allow this to happen or they may seek to intervene and create a system for explicit identification of priorities, taking into account evidence on effectiveness and cost-effectiveness and the views of the public. Chapter 5 reviews how priorities are established in practice in the Member States. Chapter 6 examines a number of theoretical ways of establishing priorities – burden of disease cost/benefit analysis, maximizing the quality of life – and describes some systematic approaches to priority setting in the European Union and elsewhere.

Member States are faced with two other areas in which they must make choices that affect the health of their populations. The first reflects growing recognition that successful responses to many of the major health scourges facing the Union lie in prevention rather than cure. Member States may choose to reorient policies towards health promotion and prevention. This will involve actions by many different sectors and will require new ways of looking at the determinants of health. Chapter 7 examines the health promotion and preventive policies adopted in Member States and the extent to which preventive actions may reduce costs through reductions in the need for curative services for Member States in the future. It shows that there are considerable opportunities to learn from the experiences of each other.

The second relates to increasing migration into and within the Union. Member States may choose to examine how they meet the health needs of their migrant communities, taking into account their specific patterns of disease and factors influencing their access to preventive and curative services. Some of the major initiatives to provide services for migrants and ethnic minorities in the Member States are described in Chapter 8.

Overall these choices aim to achieve further health improvement and to secure greater efficiency in the use of resources. They are not comprehensive and there are other approaches that have not been examined in detail. None the less, the choices described here represent some of those with most potential for collaborative action at the European level, either through Commission or inter-governmental action or through the exchange of experience. There is inevitably a degree of overlap between the categories used in this book: for example, policies whose main aim is to improve health may also contribute to cost containment and cost containment policies inevitably influence priorities. Finally, Chapter 9 sets out the future roles that can be played by the Union in helping Member States to make fundamental choices in the field of health improvement and in promoting the more efficient use of resources.

1

Challenges to Health

In future years the population of Europe will face growing challenges to health. These have been set out before, most recently in a European Commission communication on the framework for action in the field of public health.[4] They include: an ageing population, with the percentage of people aged 60 and over projected to increase from 17.5 per cent in 1980 to 24 per cent in 2010; increasing population mobility; diseases arising from environmental changes and hazards in the workplace; rising expectations concerning health; and socioeconomic problems with, in particular, social exclusion. Individually or in concert, they are associated with rising levels of some chronic diseases, increasing potential for the rapid spread of certain communicable diseases, growing numbers of migrants with specific health needs, increasing costs as a result of both ageing and demands for new technology, and the growing challenges of inequity, unemployment and social exclusion. This chapter examines the impact of some of these factors in Member States, starting with a review of trends in the most common causes of death, moving to an examination of inequalities in health and health care. It concludes with a brief examination of the needs of migrant populations within the Union. This chapter draws heavily on available data, which is largely on mortality. This has the effect of over-emphasizing those conditions from which people die and under-emphasizing many chronic diseases and, especially, mental health. This should not be interpreted as implying any judgement about the relative importance of different diseases. This issue is discussed further in Chapter 6.

Recent trends in health status and the potential for health improvement[5]

Trends in health status are examined, first, in terms of composite measures such as life expectancy and certain measures of mortality among mothers and infants. Second,

1

some of the more common causes of deaths are reviewed, focusing on the extent of variation among Member States and the potential for improvement. Third, sources of data on morbidity are examined. As will be seen, the most striking observation about the pattern of health and disease in Member States is its diversity. For example, the mean life expectancy at birth varies by almost five years. The death rates from many common diseases typically vary by a factor of two or three. This diversity provides the basis for an agenda for public health action.

Life expectancy

Life expectancy at birth provides a composite indication of health status although the explanation for any changes requires more detailed study of the causes of death among different groups. Values for each Member State are shown in Figure 1.1.

Figure 1.1: Life expectancy at birth for males and females European Union countries, 1990

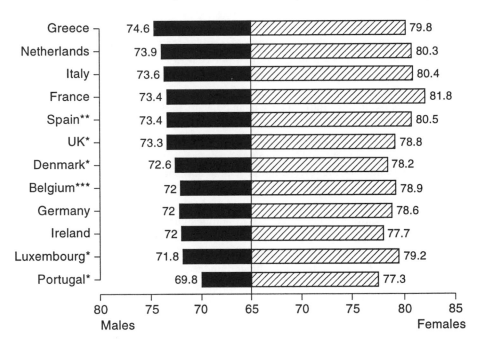

*1991 **1989 ***1987

Source: WHO Health for All Data-Base.

The difference between the highest and lowest values, for males, is 4.8 years and, for females, is 4.5 years. There are differences in the rankings for males and females, with the highest rates, for males, seen in Greece and, for females, in France.

Life expectancy at birth has increased in all EU countries between 1970 and 1990 and at broadly similar rates in each Member State (Figure 1.2). The exceptions are Denmark and Portugal. Although Denmark had one of the highest life expectancies in the Community in 1970, there has been only a slight increase in male life expectancy and no change in female life expectancy since the late 1970s. Recent work has linked this with continuing high levels of tobacco consumption. Portugal experienced a rapid rise between 1970 and 1985 although there has been a slight decline of approximately one year in the last years of the 1980s. This has been greater among men than among women and was associated with a rise in the crude death rate of 1 per 1000 between 1989 and 1991. At least some of the change was due to higher death rates from cerebrovascular disease and malignant neoplasms.

Since 1970, the highest levels of life expectancy have occurred consistently in the southern European countries, believed by some to be partly due to the Mediterranean diet consumed by their populations (see Figure 1.2).

Figure 1.2: Trends in life expectancy at birth European Union countries, 1970-91

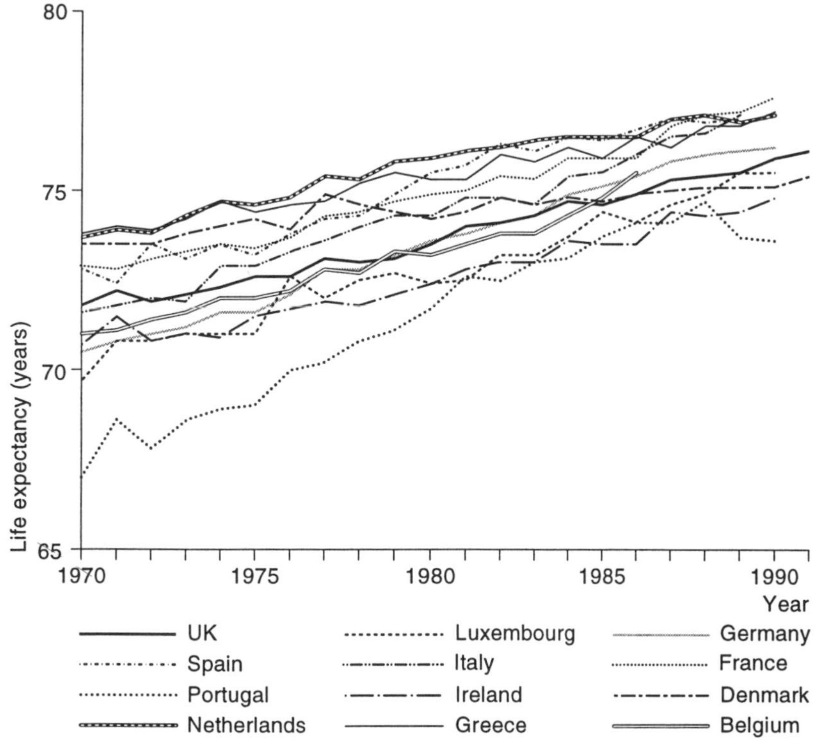

Source: WHO Health for All Data-Base.

Infant, perinatal and maternal mortality
Data for the most recent available year are shown in Table 1.1. The infant mortality rate (deaths in the first year of life per 1000 live births) largely reflects general socioeconomic conditions. All Member States have experienced decreases since 1970, with those with the highest initial levels experiencing the greatest falls. The changes in the southern European countries have been especially notable with, for example, Portugal experiencing a fall from over 50 per 1000 in 1970 to 11 per 1000 in 1990 (Figure 1.3).

**Figure 1.3: Trends in infant mortality
European Union countries, 1970-91**

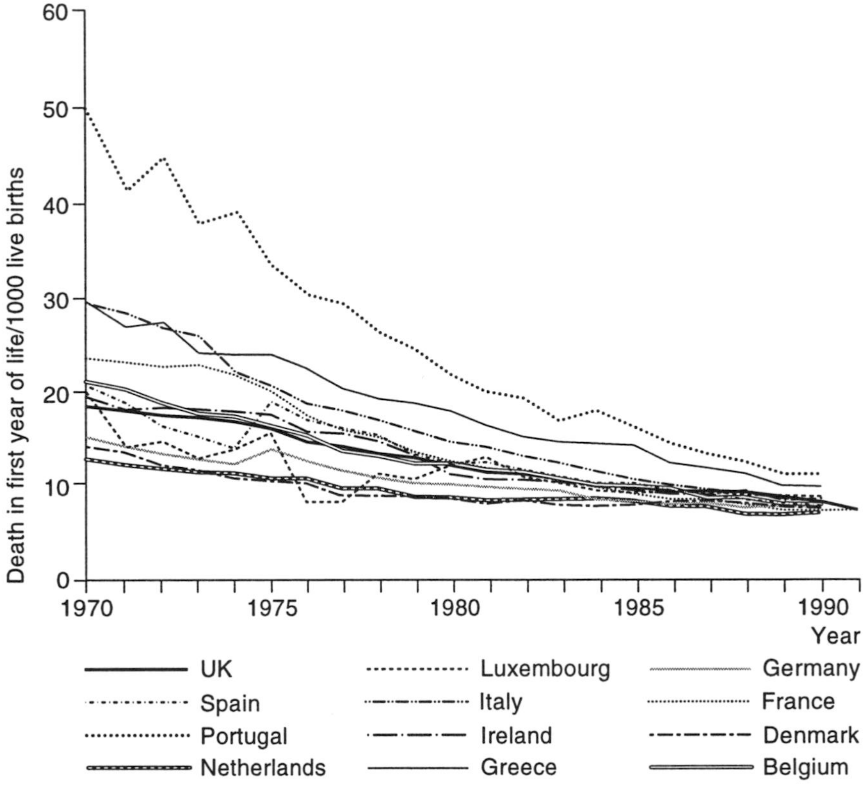

Source: WHO Health for All Data-Base.

The perinatal mortality rate (deaths in the first week of life plus stillbirths divided by all births) is a more sensitive measure of prenatal and obstetric care (see Table 1.1). It has also decreased in all Member States although substantial differences still remain with the rate in Portugal almost twice as high as that in Denmark.

Maternal deaths have fallen to very low levels in all countries, yet although numbers are small there is still a three-fold variation between Member States. There is evidence from, for example, the British Confidential Enquiry into Maternal Deaths, that many of these deaths are preventable with existing medical knowledge and technologies.

Table 1.1: Infant, perinatal and maternal mortality rates

	Infant mortality[1] (Deaths/1000 live births)		Perinatal mortality[1] (Deaths/1000 live and stillbirths)		Maternal mortality[2] (Deaths/100 000 births) 1985-89
Belgium	8.9	(1992)	11.29	(1984)	3.96*
W. Germany	6.88	(1991)	5.82	(1991)	8.18
Denmark	6.51	(1992)	8.15	(1992)	5.23
Spain	7.19	(1991)	8.30	(1989)	4.76*
France	7.26	(1991)	8.20	(1991)	9.82
Greece	9.03	(1991)	12.86	(1988)	5.38
Ireland	5.0	(1992)	10.29	(1987)	4.12
Italy	8.3	(1991)	10.41	(1991)	6.08
Luxembourg	7.19	(1991)	8.97	(1989)	4.54
Netherlands	6.29	(1992)	9.42	(1990)	7.43*
Portugal	8.73	(1993)	14.60	(1989)	9.24*
United Kingdom	6.58	(1992)	8.32	(1989)	7.78

The figures for maternal mortality are for the period 1985-89 unless otherwise stated. (* 1985-88)

Sources: 1.WHO Health for All Data-Base (1994); 2. The 3rd edition of the EC 'Atlas of avoidable deaths' (in press).

Birth weight is a major determinant of perinatal mortality. The variation in the percentage of low birth weight babies is shown in Table 1.2.

Table 1.2: Percentage of low weight births

Member State	% of births under 2500 g
Belgium	6.1*
Denmark	5.5**
France	5.3*
Germany	5.9***
Greece	6.0*
Luxembourg	4.9+
Italy	5.6***
Ireland	4.7***
The Netherlands	n/a
Portugal	5.4**
Spain	4.9***
United Kingdom	6.4*

* 1990
** 1989
*** 1988
\+ average of 1989-91

Source: OECD Health Data.

The leading causes of death

There are various composite measures of the extent to which different conditions contribute to the burden of diseases borne by a population. These permit comparisons of the total population burden from different conditions but at the expense of more detailed information on the distribution of conditions between different age groups, genders, races, and social classes. It is also possible to examine the leading causes of death for each of these groups. An example, considering only gender and age, is shown in Table 1.3. Considering all ages, the burden of mortality in Europe is dominated by deaths connected with tobacco, alcohol, diet and accidents.

Tobacco is one of the leading avoidable causes of premature mortality throughout the Union. It is the major single cause of coronary heart disease and respiratory disease. It also causes cancer of the lung, oral cavity, larynx, oesophagus, bladder and kidney. These hazards are not confined to smokers as passive exposure to tobacco smoke can cause lung cancer and is associated with an increased risk of respiratory disease in children. The babies of mothers who smoke are typically smaller than those of non-smokers.

Table 1.3: Leading causes of death by age and sex in the European Union

Age	Male	Female
under 1 year	Hypoxia, birth asphyxia & other respiratory conditions	Hypoxia, birth asphyxia & other respiratory conditions
1-4 years	Motor vehicle accidents	Motor vehicle accidents
5-9 years	Motor vehicle accidents	Motor vehicle accidents
10-14 years	Motor vehicle accidents	Motor vehicle accidents
15-19 years	Motor vehicle accidents	Motor vehicle accidents
20-24 years	Motor vehicle accidents	Motor vehicle accidents
25-29 years	Motor vehicle accidents	Motor vehicle accidents
30-34 years	Motor vehicle accidents	Suicide
35-39 years	Suicide	Breast cancer
40-44 years	Acute myocardial infarction	Breast cancer
45-49 years	Acute myocardial infarction	Breast cancer
50-54 years	Acute myocardial infarction	Breast cancer
55-59 years	Acute myocardial infarction	Breast cancer
60-64 years	Acute myocardial infarction	Breast cancer
65-69 years	Acute myocardial infarction	Acute myocardial infarction
70-74 years	Acute myocardial infarction	Acute myocardial infarction
75-79 years	Acute myocardial infarction	Acute myocardial infarction
80-84 years	Acute myocardial infarction	Acute cerebrovascular disease
over 85 years	Diseases of pulmonary circ. & other cardiopathies	Diseases of pulmonary circ. & other cardiopathies

Source: WHO Health for All Data-Base.

Although, in the Union overall, tobacco consumption has decreased slightly between 1976 and 1990, this conceals major differences between Member States, with decreases in the six Northern European countries, varying from 16.9 per cent in Denmark to 52.2 per cent in the Netherlands but increases in Southern Europe with Spain showing a rise of 83.4 per cent.

**Figure 1.4: Trends in cancer of the trachea, lung and bronchus (females)
European Union countries, 1970-91**

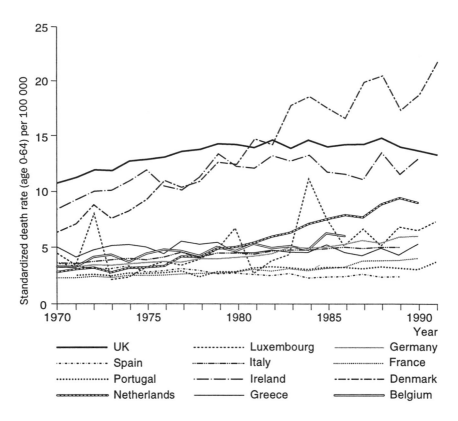

Source: WHO Health for All Data-Base.

Throughout the 1980s, Greece has consistently had the highest level of consumption in the Community and this has risen steadily from 1975 to 1987 although there has been a moderate fall since. There have also been increases in consumption in Italy and Portugal. There are also important gender differences in trends in smoking and the percentage of males and females smoking cigarettes as shown in Table 1.4. There is considerable evidence that young women are targeted particularly by tobacco advertisers. These trends have serious implications for the health of women in future decades.

The slight decrease in tobacco consumption in Northern Europe has, in most cases, had little effect on deaths from lung cancer because of the long interval between exposure to tobacco and the development of cancer. Consequently, death rates have climbed steadily throughout the 1970s and 1980s, reflecting the considerable increase in smoking in the 1960s and 1970s (Figures 1.4 & 1.5). The exceptions are

Figure 1.5: Trends in cancer of the trachea, lung and bronchus (males) European Union countries, 1970-91

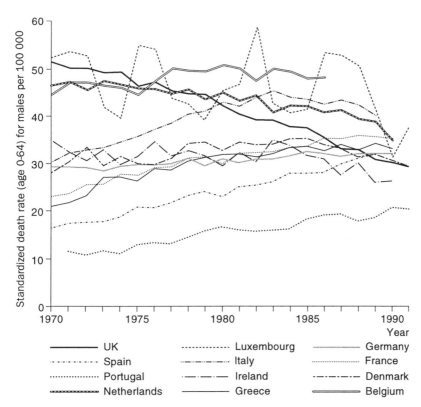

Source: WHO Health for All Data-Base.

the United Kingdom and, since the late 1980s, the Netherlands and Ireland. The death rate from lung cancer in the United Kingdom was the highest in the Community in 1970 but it has since fallen by almost one third. There are also important sex differences in many Member States, reflecting differences in tobacco consumption. For example, the dramatic decrease in deaths among British men has been offset, to some extent, by a slight increase in deaths among women in the 1970s, although this too has begun to decrease. Similarly, in the Netherlands, deaths among men from lung cancer have fallen while those among women have increased.

Although other factors are involved, such as outdoor air pollution, death rates from bronchitis, emphysema and asthma also reflect damage from exposure to tobacco. In this case, death rates have been falling in most Member States with the steepest declines in the United Kingdom, Ireland, and Portugal. In contrast, there has been a slight increase in Denmark and little change in France.

Table 1.4: Percentage of smokers

Member State	% Males 15+ smoking	% Females 15+ smoking
Belgium	42.4***	23.5***
Germany	36.3*	21.4*
Denmark	45.9¶	40.1¶
Spain	51.5**	21.4**
France	37.8*	19.2*
Greece	n/a	n/a
Luxembourg	41^	25^
Italy	40.8++	17.3++
Ireland	30.0¶	30.0¶
Netherlands	39.0*	31.0*
Portugal	33.6+	5.1+
United Kingdom	31.0*	29.0*

¶ 1992 * – 1990, ** – 1989, *** – 1988, + – 1987, ++ – 1986,
^ – 1987 based on a national sample of 1000 persons.
Source: OECD Health Data and unpublished data from OECD.

Levels of alcohol consumption reflect closely death rates from liver disease and cirrhosis and are also an important cause of motor vehicle accidents. In the period 1970 to 1988 the northern Member States have been faced with a considerable increase in alcohol consumption per head – in three countries (Denmark, Netherlands and the United Kingdom) by over 30 per cent, while those Member States with traditionally high levels (Spain, France, Italy, Luxembourg, and Portugal) have experienced declines of, for example, 33.7 per cent in Italy and 21.7 per cent in France.

Diet varies widely within Europe, reflecting traditional patterns of agriculture, access to the sea, and similar factors. As a consequence, there is great diversity in the consumption of certain components of food which are thought to be related to health and, in particular, cancer and ischaemic heart disease. Total consumption of lipids is much higher in Northern than in Southern Europe although the pattern is changing, with considerable increases in fat consumption in some countries such as Spain. Outside the European Union, in countries such as Finland[6] and the United States,[7] there have been substantial changes in the opposite direction, with associated decreases in blood cholesterol levels and the incidence of ischaemic heart disease, showing that dietary change can be effective in reducing heart disease. While total fat consumption has long been recognized to be associated with the development of ischaemic heart disease, there is growing evidence that a diet rich in certain types of fish has a substantial protective effect on heart disease.[8,9] There is also considerable evidence that diets high in fibre have a protective effect against certain forms of cancer, most notably of the colon and rectum and growing evidence of a possible preventive role against a wide range of cancers for antioxidants such as ß-carotene found in fresh fruit and vegetables.[10]

Turning to specific diseases, death rates from ischaemic heart disease have declined during the 1980s in all Member States except Greece and the former German Democratic Republic having increased throughout the 1960s and early 1970s (Figure 1.6). The declines have been most marked in those countries with the highest initial rates – Luxembourg, the Netherlands and the United Kingdom. There is considerable variation between Member States, with low levels in Southern European countries and the United Kingdom standing out from the rest with a rate that is still almost twice as high as the Union average. Although tobacco consumption is the single most important risk factor in the development of ischaemic heart disease, there are many other factors involved, most notably diet, but also blood pressure, family history, and diabetes.

**Figure 1.6: Trends in ischaemic heart disease
European Union countries, 1970-91**

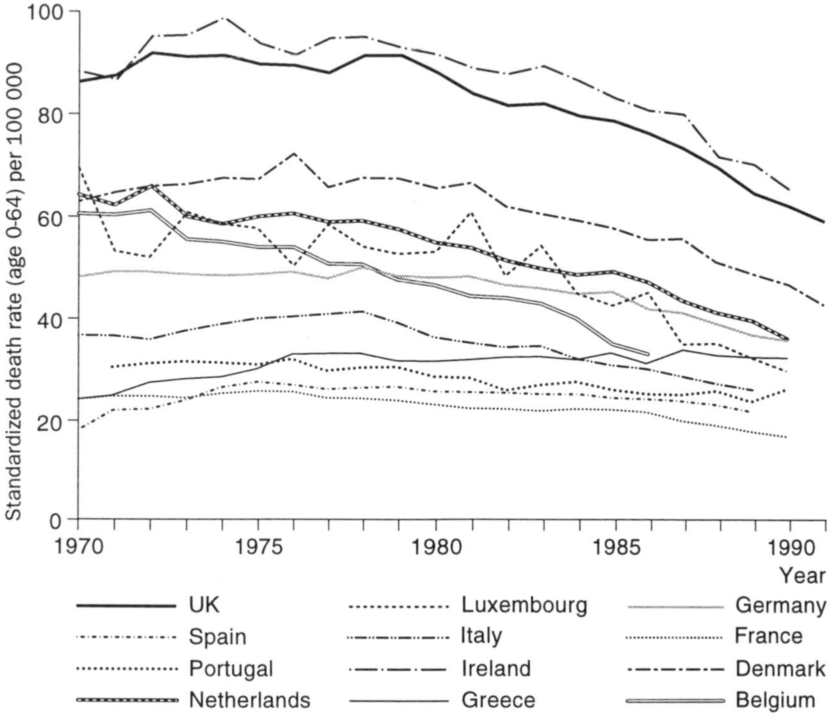

———— UK	············· Luxembourg	~~~~~~ Germany
·–··–····· Spain	·–··–····· Italy	·············· France
················ Portugal	·—··—··— Ireland	·–··–···· Denmark
▰▰▰▰▰ Netherlands	———— Greece	═══════ Belgium

Source: WHO Health for All Data-Base.

In the case of cerebrovascular disease, all Member States (except the former German Democratic Republic) have experienced decreases in death rates since 1970 but, again, those Member States with the highest initial rates have experienced the greatest declines (Figure 1.7). As with ischaemic heart disease, considerable differences remain in terms of absolute rates, with the highest levels seen in Portugal. It is thought that this may be associated with the high salt content of the Portuguese diet.

Figure 1.7: Trends in cerebrovascular disease
European Union countries, 1970-91

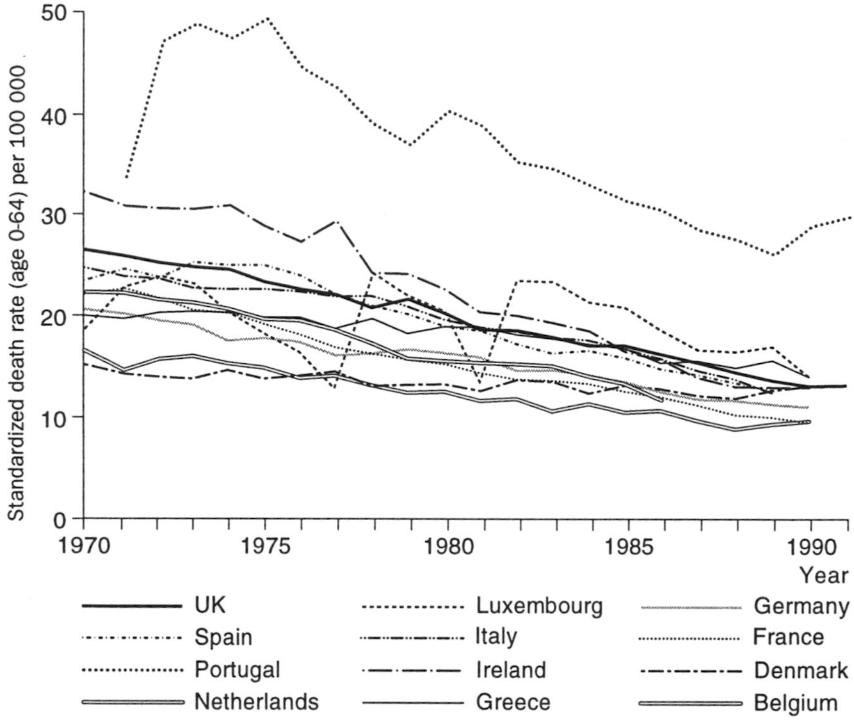

———— UK	············ Luxembourg	———— Germany
··········· Spain	—··—··— Italy	··············· France
··············· Portugal	—·—·— Ireland	—··—··— Denmark
———— Netherlands	———— Greece	———— Belgium

Source: WHO Health for All Data-Base.

Death rates from motor vehicle accidents have fallen in all Member States, except Spain, although there is still an almost threefold variation, with the highest rate in Portugal and the lowest rates in Denmark, the Netherlands, and the United Kingdom. These crude statistics obscure an even greater variation in the extent to which different age groups are affected. For example, while the total death rate from motor vehicle accidents in the United Kingdom is relatively low, it has one of the highest rates in the European Union for deaths among child pedestrians.

Death rates from cervical cancer vary widely. Member States can be divided into those whose levels during the 1970s were high (Germany, Denmark, Luxembourg, the Netherlands, Portugal and the United Kingdom), medium (Belgium, France and Ireland) and low (Spain, Greece and Italy) (Figure 1.8). Known risk factors include sexual activity and smoking. Those Member States with high initial levels have experienced considerable decreases, those with medium rates have experienced only slight decreases, and those with low initial rates have experienced little change or a slight increase.

Death rates from breast cancer vary almost twofold within the Union (Figure 1.9). They are associated with early menarche, late menopause and age at first full-term pregnancy. The highest rates are seen in Belgium, Denmark, Ireland, the Netherlands and the United Kingdom. The lowest rate is seen in Greece. Death rates have been increasing in all Member States, although the increases are most rapid in those with relatively low initial rates.

Figure 1.8: Trends in cervical cancer European Union countries, 1970-91

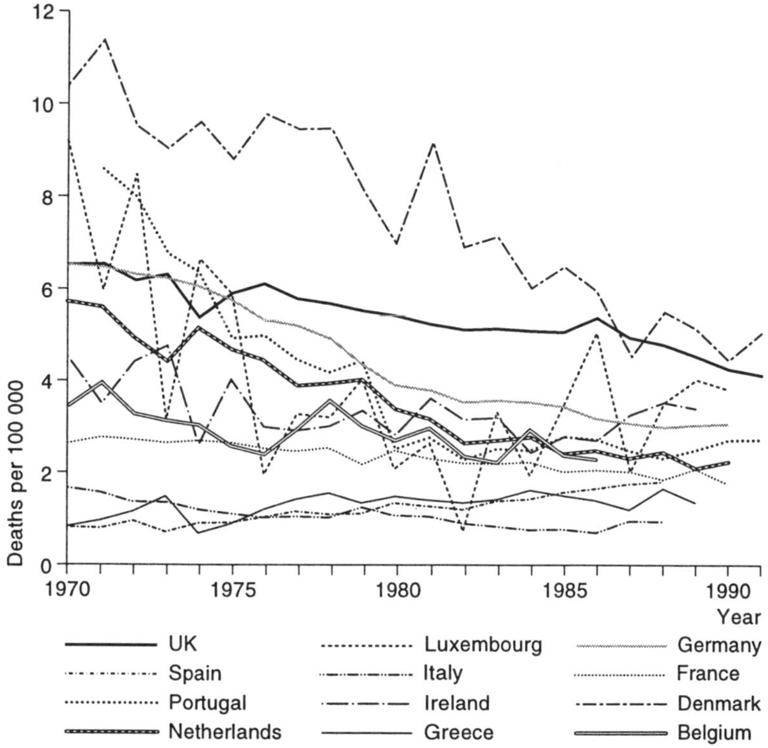

Source: WHO Health for All Data-Base.

Figure 1.9: Trends in breast cancer
European Union countries, 1970-91

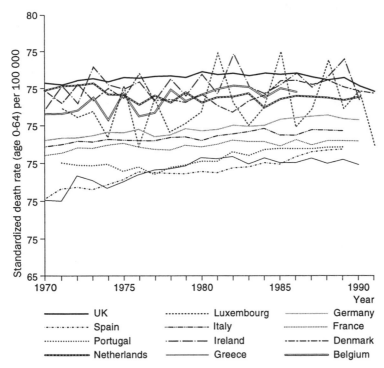

Source: WHO Health for All Data-Base.

Death rates from suicide and self-inflicted injury have been increasing in all Member States although, since 1981, there has been a considerable decline in Denmark albeit from a high level.

Deaths from cancer of the gastrointestinal tract also vary widely although, as with some other diseases, trend analysis is complicated by the change of versions of the International Classification of Disease in the late 1970s. Death rates vary almost twofold, with the highest rates seen in the Southern European countries and, especially, Portugal, Spain and Italy, and the lowest rate in Denmark. This is somewhat puzzling as there is a growing body of evidence that a diet rich in fruit and vegetables is protective.[11]

There have been rapid increases in the rate of skin cancer in many Northern European countries. This is largely due to increasing exposure to the sun, partly as a result of taking more holidays in areas such as the Mediterranean.

Deaths associated with important surgical conditions (appendicitis, intestinal obstruction and hernia) have fallen dramatically in all Member States and are now at very low levels everywhere.

Measures of morbidity

As illustrated above, international comparisons of health status have traditionally focused on measures of mortality as the information is easily available and is collected in a relatively standardized form. It is, however, at best incomplete as a reflection of the health status of a population. Unfortunately, comparisons based on morbidity are much more difficult, partly because of the lack of consistent definitions and also because many possible measures, such as hospital admission rates, are as much a measure of supply as of demand. There are a few exceptions. All Member States have mechanisms for collecting information on certain communicable diseases either through an obligatory notification system or, as is often the case with HIV/AIDS, through voluntary systems. Cancer registries provide a further source of data although the completeness of coding varies considerably and there are still many parts of the Union where they do not exist. This is particularly a problem in Member States where data protection legislation precludes linkage of data, as in several German Länder. There are also a series of initiatives, many with Commission support through programmes such as BIOMED, collecting comparative data on specific conditions. Examples include EUROCAT, with a focus on congenital abnormalities, studies of chronic obstructive pulmonary disease, occupational cancer, cerebrovascular disease,[12] and a planned data-base on road accidents.[13]

Although the absolute numbers are relatively small, one communicable disease requires specific attention. The incidence of HIV/AIDS has increased rapidly since the early 1980s in all Member States, but at differing rates. The most recent available figures for incidence of AIDS are shown in Table 1.5. AIDS is of particular importance at a Union level because of its increasing incidence, the absence of a vaccine or a cure, the potential impact of increasing mobility on future incidence, and the scope for prevention.

The data presented in Table 1.5 indicate that mortality and morbidity data can give some idea of the relative extent of different challenges to health but they are not, on their own, sufficient to generate priorities. They take no account of levels of disability or impairment. For example, many services, particularly for the elderly, aim to relieve pain and improve the quality of life rather than save lives. In the case of asthma, what matters is not just deaths or even prevalence, but the severity of the condition. Patient outcome is not just a matter of looking at deaths: a package of measures is needed including impairment, disability and handicap.

The limitations of existing mortality and morbidity data are seen more clearly when considering drug abuse, the one major health scourge facing the Union that is mentioned specifically in the Maastricht Treaty. Indirect measures of the impact of drug abuse include the incidence of HIV/AIDS or hepatitis B, levels of crime, and the street prices of drugs. The last of these are used in some Member States as a measure of supply as they vary inversely with the supply of drugs. The indirect nature of these relationships, the many factors involved in reducing drug abuse, and the absence of internationally comparable data make it impossible to compare directly the impact of illicit drugs and the effect of policies in different Member States.[14]

**Table 1.5: AIDS cases and incidence rates per million population
European Union**

Country	Year of Diagnosis				Cumulative total 1987 to mid year 1993
	1987		1992		
	Cases	Incidence	Cases	Incidence	Cases
				(per million)	
Belgium	120	12.1	221	22.1	1411
Denmark	100	19.6	197	37.9	1225
France	2232	40.1	4439	78.0	25459
Germany	1078	13.9	1403	17.4	9997
Greece	53	5.3	162	15.7	800
Ireland	20	5.7	77	22.0	341
Italy	1016	17.7	3937	67.9	17864
Luxembourg	3	7.5	12	30.0	67
Netherlands	241	16.5	481	31.6	2678
Portugal	72	7.0	281	26.8	1307
Spain	1020	26.2	3815	98.8	19815
United Kingdom	669	11.8	1330	23.0	7699
TOTAL	6624	-	16355	-	88663

Note: Diagnosis reported by December 1987 and December 1992 and cumulative total, unadjusted for reporting delays (1987-93).

Source: WHO – EC Collaborating Centre on AIDS, *AIDS Surveillance in the European Community Countries*, Paris, 1993.

The preceding paragraphs have focused on specific causes of death and disease. There is, however, an increasing recognition of the need to tackle some of the underlying factors that determine levels of a wide range of differing diseases. The most important is inequality.

Inequalities in health and health services

The first of WHO's targets for Health for All by the Year 2000 is the reduction of health inequalities. By the year 2000 'the actual differences in health status between countries and between groups within countries should be reduced by at least 25 per cent'.[15]

It is important to distinguish between inequalities in *health* and in *health services*. Inequalities in health refer to differences in the 'outcomes' of policies or the lack of them: that is, differences in health status, as measured by, for example, life-expectancy, mortality rates, or morbidity rates. Inequalities in health care refers to differences in what can be thought of as the 'inputs' to health services – doctors, nurses, or hospital beds, service utilization rates, health care expenditures, etc.

Not all inequalities in health are necessarily inequitable. According to one definition, inequalities in health are differences which are unnecessary, avoidable and judged to be unjust and unfair.[16] Thus biological variations do not fall into this category nor does health-damaging behaviour if it is freely chosen such as smoking or participation in certain sports and pastimes. Similarly, inequalities in the provision of health services may be justified by greater need – particularly among the lower socioeconomic groups.

Also, the objectives of policy with respect to health or health care are – or should be – derivative of core or fundamental objectives of social and economic organization, such as the promotion of social justice, the attainment of economic efficiency, and the preservation of individual liberty. Achieving any or all of these might require certain inequalities in areas of social policy such as health, rather than full equality. For instance, the promotion of economic efficiency might require that health (and health care) be concentrated on the more productive members of society and less on, say, the elderly or the disabled. Social justice might require the reverse.

How far is concern about inequality in health and health care shared among Member States? Whitehead suggests that interest in the debate on health and health care inequalities appears to be relatively low in Germany and France, moderate in Italy and high in Spain (particularly with respect to inequalities in health care) and Portugal (with respect to primary care[17]). In the United Kingdom, the debate outside of government is intense; but the Government itself does not appear to see these kind of issues as a very high priority, at least until recently. In the Netherlands there is political support for the development of strategies to reduce inequalities, and in Sweden all national policy agencies are required to report on specific goals to reduce health inequalities and on the impact of their other policies on these inequalities.[18]

The extent of inequality
The problems associated with measuring the extent of, first, inequalities in *health,* can be categorized under the headings of *health indicators* and *inequality between whom*? So far as *health indicators* are concerned, most existing European research concentrates heavily on mortality rates, with some side-glances at self-reported morbidity. There are well-known problems with these as indicators of health (and ill-health), and there is a need for further indicators to supplement existing analyses. On *inequality between whom,* it is necessary first to separate out the questions of inequality *between* Member States and inequality *within* Member States. The

former is discussed in other sections of the book. Inequality within Member States can be found along a number of different dimensions – in particular, population, region, socioeconomic status, gender and ethnicity. In the case of *population* inequality, the variation in the age of death has been calculated in OECD countries by using inequality measures such as the Gini coefficient for the distribution of age-at-death for each country.[19] The study found substantial differences between Member States; if the set of countries was divided into thirds according to the value of the Gini coefficient, Luxembourg, Netherlands and the component countries of the UK were in the lowest third with the least inequality, Belgium, Germany, Denmark and Italy in the middle third, and the remainder of EU countries in the highest third with the greatest inequality.

Some of the studies on *regional* and *social* inequalities in health within Member States show wide variations.[20,21,22] For instance, in Italy, there have been widening differentials in infant health between the South and the rest of the country, while in Denmark, there are few significant regional differences in infant mortality, and in Britain, regional inequalities for all younger age groups are diminishing.[23] Inequalities in adult health by socioeconomic status have apparently been widening in France, the Netherlands and the United Kingdom.[24] In the United Kingdom, the widening gap has been due, at least in part, to actual increases in mortality among the least well off.[25] They also appear to have been diminishing in Denmark. This last finding is encouraging, since it suggests that 'inequalities in health should not be interpreted as an unavoidable 'natural law' but as open to change by public health intervention'.[26]

A comparison of inequalities in health within certain countries has been undertaken, using standard data and methods.[27,28] Comparisons are available for both mortality and morbidity, and are summarized below[29] (Box 1.1). They show interesting differences and underline the importance of using both mortality and morbidity indicators. The use of all-cause mortality conceals a picture of even greater complexity as there are considerable differences in the causes of death in different social classes.[30] Consequently actions directed at a particular cause of death may have the effect of increasing inequality.

Similarly, in the eight Member States for which data have been assembled, there are social inequalities in both the provision and finance of health care, but again their magnitudes and direction vary.[31] With respect to finance, a European Community funded study found that primarily tax-financed systems such as those operating in Denmark, Ireland, Portugal and the United Kingdom, tend to be mildly progressive, whereas social insurance systems, such as those in France and the Netherlands tend to be regressive. With respect to health care delivery, the apparent extent of inequality in each country is very sensitive to the method of measurement chosen. However, it appears safe to conclude that in Spain and the United Kingdom, despite their universal and comprehensive public systems, there is unequal treatment for equal need, with the direction of inequality favouring the better-off. By way of contrast, the Netherlands, where public cover is more limited, and income-related, appears to have a neutral distribution.

Box 1.1: Differences in mortality and morbidity by social class

Mortality		*Morbidity*	
Low	Netherlands	*Low*	Norway
	Denmark		Sweden
	Norway		United Kingdom
	Sweden		Spain
Medium low	Finland	*Medium*	Netherlands
	United Kingdom		Denmark
			Finland
Medium high	Germany		Germany
	United States		
		High	Italy
High	France		United States
	Italy		

Source: Mackenbach J.P., Kunst A.E., *Health and social inequality in Europe,* British Medical Journal, Vol. 309, 1994, p.57.

The causes of inequalities in health and health services

Perhaps the most comprehensive national investigation of health inequalities was the Black Report[32] on the United Kingdom published in 1980. It considered four possible explanations of health inequalities: artefact, natural or social selection, materialist and cultural/behavioural. The first concerns statistical issues: is any apparent inequality simply a consequence of the method of measurement used? The second concerns the direction of causation in the relationship between health and inequality: are unhealthy individuals in a lower social class, ill because they are in that class, or are they in that class because they are ill? The materialist explanation is that inequalities in health are determined by the fundamental inequalities in resources and power in the society; while the cultural/behavioural explanation is that they are determined by differences between the classes in individuals' behaviour concerning health-damaging or health-promoting activities. Of all of these, the Report favoured the third, arguing that, overall, 'it is our belief that it is in some form or forms of the 'materialist' approach that the best answer lies'.[33]

In practice, however, people's behaviour is greatly influenced by the material constraints they face on their activities. The outcomes of the choices they make will partly be a function of their tastes or preferences; but will also depend heavily on their constraints (such as their income). Moreover, even their tastes may be in part determined by their, or their parents', constraints. Thus one would expect poverty to be a cause of ill-health.

Figure 1.10 shows that the Member States where relative poverty was increasing over the period 1975 to 1985 had lower increases in life expectancy than other Member States. Other data does not, however, support this conclusion. Individuals brought up in poor households whose parents found it cheaper to buy white bread rather than brown, or to smoke a packet of cigarettes rather than take a walk in the country, are likely to develop tastes that accord with their situation. Hence explanations for health inequities in terms of behavioural differences are not necessarily alternatives for explanations which rely on differences in the socioeconomic environment: rather, behaviour may be one of the routes through which environmental influences work.

There is considerable evidence that within countries, there is a link between socioeconomic circumstances and health.[34] However, the exact mechanism is not always clear. Also, there is a puzzle that, whatever the situation within countries, *between* countries above a GDP of about US$7000, there is no very obvious relationship between income and health at a national level.[35] A possible explanation for this may be found in recent work relating *inequalities* in income (within countries) to *average* levels of health at a national level.[36]

Figure 1.10: Annual changes in poverty and life expectancy European Union countries, 1975-85

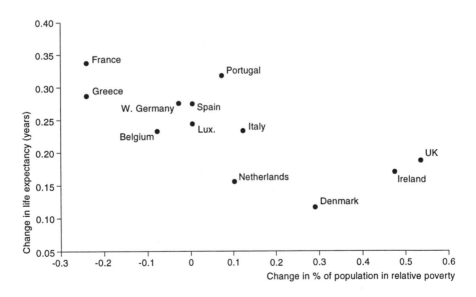

Source: Wilkinson R.G., *Income distribution and life expectancy,* British Medical Journal, Vol. 304, 1992, pp.165-8.

There has been no overall study of the reasons for differences between social groups in their utilization of health care services. This may be because, as was discussed earlier, it has yet to be established to everyone's satisfaction that such inequalities exist. If, for the sake of argument, it is assumed that they do exist, then there are a number of possible explanations. These include: the absence of medical facilities in poorer areas; the poor having worse access to such facilities as do exist, due to their possessing few cars and telephones (and hence finding it more difficult to make or keep appointments); manual workers, unlike the salaried middle class, losing money when they take time off work to go to the doctor; and failures of communication between essentially middle-class medical staff and working-class patients. Of these, some are under the control of health services (relocation of medical facilities); some are more likely to be affected by changes in the overall income distribution, through taxation and social protection policies; some, such as communication difficulties between the classes, may not be amenable to any short-term remedy.

For policy purposes, it is obviously important to establish which of these factors, if any, are the most important. However, it seems unlikely that anything can be done using published data. New data are required, possibly from surveys of the kind discussed in the previous section. Overall, this seems to be an important field for research and policy, but one that is currently relatively uncultivated.

Policy
As the above suggests there is considerable uncertainty about the causes of many of the inequalities in health and health care, and hence it is not always obvious at which point policy interventions are likely to be effective. Some forms of intervention may in fact make things worse; a recent study of health immunization programmes found a higher take-up among the rich than the poor, leading to greater inequalities in both health and health care.[37] However, some interventions do seem to work, particularly at work place level. In general, there is a need for extensive study of the effect of different institutional structures on inequalities in health and health care, and here comparisons between Member States could be of great value. Different countries have different institutions and experiences of inequalities in health and health care; hence each offers the possibility of acting as a 'laboratory' for the others.

Summary

This chapter has explored some of the major health challenges facing Member States. These include widely varying levels of health status and of specific diseases, in-equity in health and health care, and the specific needs of migrants. Although the pattern of challenges facing each Member State is different, many of the solutions will be common, with great scope to learn from successful policies elsewhere. Member States must make certain choices about how to respond to these challenges. The following chapter will explore the health services context in which these choices are made.

2

The Health Care Context

This chapter provides an overview of the ways in which health services are organized and financed within Member States, the levels of health care expenditure, the resulting patterns of provision and utilization, and the way in which they are perceived by the public.

The patterns of health service organization adopted in different countries are the result of the interaction between political, historical, cultural and socioeconomic factors. Ultimately, these reflect broader societal values and the relative weights assigned to different social objectives such as equity, efficiency or the merits of individual freedom versus collectivism. Similarly, the levels of health care expenditure, the provision of inputs and the use of resources between different sectors of spending, such as primary versus secondary care, in each Member State are indicative of the relative value assigned to health care against other competing sectors, as well as of the priorities attributed to different health care interventions and client groups.

The organization and financing of health care

In all Member States, except the Netherlands, compulsory health insurance as defined by the International Labour Office covers over 85 per cent of the population. Universal rights (or the same rights for all citizens) to health care have been extended over the past fifteen years until they are to be found in six of the 12 Member States – Denmark, Greece, Ireland, Italy, Portugal and the United Kingdom. In Greece, the universal right consists only of access to public hospitals including their out-patient departments. In Ireland, only those with low incomes are covered for primary care (the General Medical Services scheme): those not covered have to pay for care received privately and a modest amount per day for hospital care received publicly. The Netherlands has been exploring ways of moving towards universal care and virtually all those not compulsorily covered are members of voluntary insurance schemes. Provision for serious and prolonged disability and sickness have long been universal and, from 1992, pharmaceuticals and some smaller services were added: only about 60 per cent of the population is compulsorily covered for hospital and specialist services. Very nearly universal rights (about 99 per cent coverage) are now found in Belgium, France, Luxembourg and Spain and over 90 per cent are covered by the statutory insurers in Germany. But in Belgium the self-employed and employers are only covered for the heavy risks – in-patient care and for certain diseases such as cancer and tuberculosis. Those not covered are the very poor, immigrants and the wealthy. Where coverage is not universal, voluntary health insurance fills most of the gaps left by statutory insurance.

The Member States fall into three main groups:

The Netherlands	financed by a mixture of social and private insurance with mainly private providers.
Belgium, France, Germany and Luxembourg	financed mainly by social insurance with mixed public and private providers.
Denmark, Spain, Greece, Ireland, Italy, Portugal and United Kingdom	financed mainly by taxation, with mainly public providers.

There are a number of different insurance funds providing compulsory insurance in Greece, Belgium, Germany, France, Luxembourg, the Netherlands and Portugal, but with the exception of Greece, Portugal and to some extent Germany, they all provide, as a minimum, the same benefits in the same way and pay providers the same negotiated rates. In Germany, Greece and Portugal, there are also special funds for particular occupational groups which may provide benefits in different ways – for example, in the way doctors are paid. There are about 1100 separate funds in Germany, nine in Luxembourg and five federations of funds in Belgium. In Greece, 84 per cent of the population are covered by two funds and in France 75 per cent of the population is in one fund. Germany is currently reducing the number of funds.

Even where rights to health care are not based on the payment of insurance contributions, the latter may still be collected and used for the health services as in Greece, Italy and the United Kingdom. Only in Denmark and Portugal are services wholly financed from taxation. The majority of health care for the compulsorily insured is financed from insurance contributions in Germany, France, Luxembourg and the Netherlands. The proportion of expenditure financed in this way is about half in Belgium, under half in Spain, Greece and Italy and only about 10 per cent in the United Kingdom.

Table 2.1 shows in outline the main systems of supplying services in the 12 countries. The Table refers to the main scheme or, in the case of Ireland and the Netherlands, to the scheme for the lower income groups and, in the case of Greece, to the largest scheme for those in regular employment. It does not necessarily follow that finance from governmental budgets leads to services being owned by government and all staff working in the health service being salaried to government. In fact this model is only to be found in Portugal and Greece (for the two largest schemes) and partly in Spain. And, in the last two countries, private services are contracted to supplement those owned by insurers. It does not follow that a public hospital is necessarily financed even to a predominant extent directly by government. This is the case in Denmark, Spain, Ireland, Italy, Portugal, the United Kingdom and partly in Greece. In the remaining countries public hospitals rely mainly or wholly on revenue from health insurers and are in competition with private hospitals.

The Table also indicates the method of paying primary health care doctors. In four countries they are paid on a capitation basis, in two by salary, in four by fee-for-service, though France also has about 2000 health centres with salaried doctors and there is an option of continued salaried service in the Eastern Länder of Germany. Denmark has a mixture of capitation and fee-for-service payment for all general practitioners and Spain has some general practitioners paid by capitation and some mainly by salary. Doctors have to accept the negotiated rate of payment in all Member States, except in Luxembourg up to 1992 and France. In the latter, about a third of out-of-hospital doctors have opted to be able to charge extra. Their patients are only reimbursed a fixed percentage of the negotiated fee: in return for this status, the doctors have to pay for their own pensions and observe other conditions.

Eight Member States have specific restrictions on doctors entering insurance practice or the two main insurance schemes in Greece. In Denmark, it is the responsibility of each county to indicate which parts of their county are open or closed for the entry of further specialists and general practitioners. In Ireland, the Health Boards limit entry of general practitioners to the General Medical Services scheme for lower income patients and in Italy, control is exercised by each of the local health units. Entry to General Medical Services general practice in Ireland is highly competitive and requires formal training in general practice. This is often obtained in the United Kingdom. In Spain and Portugal, the number of posts for doctors is controlled. In Spain entry to health insurance requires, in practice, a postgraduate qualification. In Portugal, no new posts for doctors were allowed between 1986 and 1989. In Germany, the number of doctors allowed to enter insurance practice is controlled by the Regional Doctors' Associations which issue licences for insurance practice in particular specialties. In the Netherlands, an attempt was made to limit the number of doctors working but the attempt failed. In the United Kingdom, since the start of the National Health Service, entry to general practice in over-doctored areas has been heavily restricted, although there are also incentives to practise in some remote areas, such as the Scottish islands. There has been no attempt to place an overall limit on general practitioners entering the National Health Service. Entry to practise under health insurance or the health service is open to all doctors in Belgium, France, Luxembourg, and the Netherlands.

Table 2.1: Principal methods of providing services in the EU
(Main scheme or scheme for lower income persons)

Country	Direct (employed)	Indirect (contracted)	Payment of primary care doctors
Belgium		all services	fee-for-service
Germany		all services	normally fee-for-service
Denmark	hospitals	GPs, specialists outside hospitals, most dentists and physiotherapists	28% capitation 63% fee-for-service, 9% other
Spain	specialists, hospitals, GPs	pharmacies, dentists and private hospitals	60% GPs salary plus capitation 40% GPs capitation
France		all services	fee-for-service
Greece	doctors, dentists, hospitals	pharmacies, few private hospitals	salary
Ireland	public hospitals, specialists	private non-profit hospitals, GPs, pharmacies	capitation
Italy	public hospitals, specialists	private hospitals, GPs and private specialists	capitation
Luxembourg		all services	fee-for-service
Netherlands		all services	capitation
Portugal	GPs, some specialists, public hospitals	private hospitals, pharmacies, labs. for X- ray and pathology	salary
UK	public hospitals, community services	GPs, private hospitals, most dentists	capitation*

* In the United Kingdom, there are also components of salary, some fees-for-services and bonuses for achieving certain preventive targets.

Specialists serving compulsorily insured out-patients are salaried in Spain, Greece, Portugal, the United Kingdom and under the General Medical Services scheme in Ireland. In the other Member States, some or all are paid on a fee-for-service basis. In Belgium, Germany, France, Luxembourg, and the Netherlands, patients can go direct to a specialist and Greece has plans to make this possible. In the other Member States access is normally by referral from a general practitioner.

Hospital beds are over 90 per cent publicly owned in Denmark and the United Kingdom, between 80 and 90 per cent publicly owned in Italy and Portugal, and the majority are publicly owned in Spain, France, Greece and Ireland. Only about half are publicly owned in Germany and about one third are in non-profit hospitals. In Belgium, Luxembourg and the Netherlands most of the acute hospitals are private, often not-for-profit. In Belgium and Luxembourg, the Netherlands and in private hospitals in France, the doctor is normally separately paid for services rendered to in-patients. Elsewhere, the hospital pays its doctors.

In nine Member States, the insurers pay the providers for the main services to insured persons. In the remaining three, Belgium, France and Luxembourg, the cost of services outside hospital are reimbursed in part on the basis of receipted bills submitted to the insurer, while other bills are paid direct by the insurer to the provider.

Member States vary in the extent to which particular services are covered by insurance. Dentistry is provided by salaried dentists on a very limited scale in Greece under the main scheme for the urban population and also in Ireland under the General Medical Services, and in Italy and Portugal under their national health services. In Spain and the United Kingdom, dentists paid on a capitation basis provide extractions and preventive services to children. Elsewhere, dentistry is provided mainly or exclusively by dentists paid, at least in part, on a fee-for-service basis. Dentures are provided free in Luxembourg to people who have been examined in both of the last two years. In Denmark, dentistry is only partly paid for in the case of persons over the age of 18. In Italy, patients must pay for dentures but at low rates. In the other Member States there is considerable co-payment for dental care. But dentures have never been provided under the scheme in Belgium and spectacles are not reimbursable for adults except for those with very bad sight; children under 12 are entitled to free lenses and a cash grant towards the frames. From 1985, the right of adults to receive spectacles under the British National Health Service was removed unless they had special eye problems or were receiving social assistance. In Ireland, standard frames or frames up to a limited value are provided free under the General Medical Services scheme. In the other Member States there are modest grants towards the cost of spectacles or part payment for a limited range.

Variations in the utilization of health resources

There are enormous difficulties in achieving complete comparability in assembling data on the use of health resources between the different Member States. International comparisons are as good as the data on which they are based. The administrative and statistical systems in the Member States differ, and the data collected is designed to serve the more specific needs of individual health care systems rather than comparative purposes. There are substantial differences between definitions of variables, terminologies employed and methods of collection. In addition, data inaccuracies may affect the reliability of the information.

Expenditure comparisons face difficulties in drawing the boundaries of health expenditure. For instance, health expenditure statistics in different Member States vary in the extent to which they include programmes financed by agencies or Ministries other than the Ministry of Health such as those for military personnel, school health services or occupational health. Further, there are variations in the extent to which services for the elderly and chronically ill are included. There are particular difficulties in drawing a line between health expenditure and expenditure on social welfare services. When attempts are made to break down health expenditure by category, the problem of comparability becomes even more important. The most crucial problems are the boundaries between in-patient and out-patient care and between hospitals and other types of institution. In Greece, for example, out-patient health centres were, until recently, financed via hospital budgets and thus were classified as in-patient expenditure. There are also problems in comparing health service inputs and activity indicators between countries. For instance, the definition of a 'qualified nurse' differs between Member States. Definitions of hospital beds are even more variable. Measures of activity are often dictated by payment methods and these vary both within countries and within a single country over time. For example, much of the apparent increase in activity in the United Kingdom National Health Service between 1990 and 1993 was probably due to changes in the way data were collected.[38] Hospital statistics present problems of validity in almost every Member State.

Three main approaches to process and compare international data have been identified.[39] First, an international agency defines a common set of variables and collects the data accordingly through survey. Second, different countries cooperate towards harmonizing data and provide it to a single unit for compilation and comparison. Third, a common analyst collects data routinely available from country sources and tries to adapt it to common units of comparison.

The data employed in this section are based on the OECD 1993 data file, which belongs to the third group. Thus, despite the attempts to overcome the problems of comparability, these data are inevitably fraught with problems due to organizational inconsistencies, gaps in coverage, and definitional heterogeneity. There are, however, no better alternatives and as Poullier points out, 'in international comparisons, the trade-off of precision for timely accessibility of data is a difficult but a necessary one'.[40]

Health care expenditure
There are major differences in expenditures on health care. Figure 2.1 shows that the highest spending countries in terms of purchasing power parities are Germany

(US$1659) and France (US$1650) which spend about four time (Greece) and about one and half times that of the Europea (US$1154). Belgium, Italy, Luxembourg, and the Netherlands a average. Spain, Ireland and Portugal are together with Greece am spending countries in the EU.

**Figure 2.1: Per capita health spending
European Union countries, 1991**

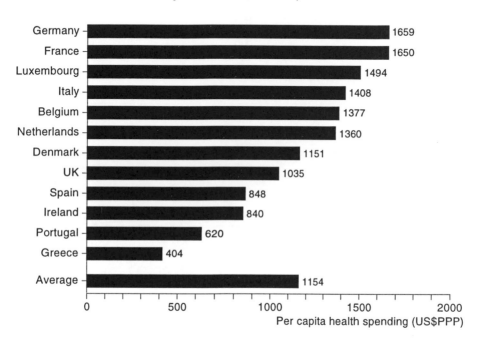

Note: US$ in purchasing power parities.

Source: OECD Health Data Version 1.5 (1993).

Even when the expenditures are expressed as a percentage of gross domestic product (GDP), large disparities remain (see Table 2.2 below). France is the highest with 9.1 per cent of GDP devoted to health care followed by Germany, Italy, the Netherlands and Belgium with shares of GDP expenditure above the EU average of 7.4 per cent. At the other end, Greece spends 5.2 per cent of GDP. Despite the well known association between national income and health care expenditure (total and as a percentage of GDP), this pattern does not wholly reflect the wealth of the countries concerned. Relatively wealthy countries, such as Denmark and the United Kingdom, spend less as a proportion of GDP than poorer countries such as Ireland and Portugal.

Table 2.2: Health care expenditure in Member States, 1991

Country	Total expenditure as percentage of GDP	Public expenditure as percentage of total
France	9.1	73.9
Germany	8.5	71.8
Italy	8.3	77.5
Netherlands	8.3	73.1
Belgium	7.9	88.9
Ireland	7.3	75.8
Luxembourg	7.2	91.4*
Portugal	6.8	61.7*
Spain	6.7	82.2
UK	6.6	83.3
Denmark	6.5	81.5
Greece	5.2	77.0*
EU average	7.4	78.2

* 1990

Source: OECD Health Data.

During recent decades several factors have combined to exert upward pressure on health expenditure in all Member States. Older populations have higher levels of chronic diseases and disability. The additional costs are falling, increasingly, on a smaller population of working age. Costs have also increased because of the growing number of conditions for which treatments or cure are available, such as chemotherapy for childhood leukaemia and certain solid tumours, the availability of new treatments that have replaced or supplemented existing treatments, such as thrombolytic drugs for myocardial infarction, and new techniques for diagnosis and treatment, such as minimally-invasive surgery. Finally, the diffusion of drugs and technology from tertiary centres has greatly increased the access to, and thus their utilization. The consequences of the changes can be seen in Figure 2.2 which indicates trends in total health care expenditure as a proportion of gross domestic product in Member States from 1961 to 1991. After rapid increases in the first two decades, the proportion grew much more slowly between 1981 and 1991 in all countries except Greece and Italy. In Germany, Denmark and Ireland, health care expenditure as a proportion of GDP fell and there were only very small increases in Luxembourg and the Netherlands. Between 1986 to 1991 health care expenditure as a proportion of GDP decreased slightly in Greece and increased slightly in Portugal. Since 1986, the figures have increased steadily in Spain coinciding with a period of economic growth and development of health services. The UK contained health care expenditure as a proportion of GDP from 1981 until 1990, after which it increased by 0.4 per cent coinciding with the introduction of the reforms of the National Health Service. In Belgium the proportion increased from 1981 to 1986: after being constant from 1986 to 1990, it increased again by 0.3 per cent in 1991. In the last decade, percentages of GDP devoted to health expenditure have increased substantially in France (1.2 per cent) and Italy – 1.4 per cent since 1986.

Figure 2.2: Health expenditure as a proportion of GDP European Union countries, 1961-91

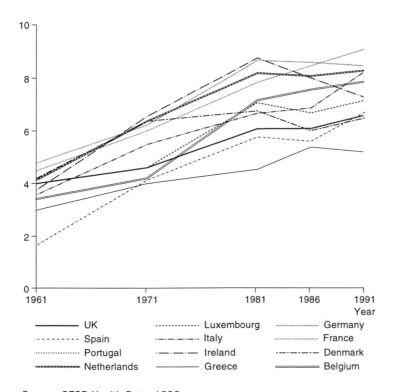

Source: OECD Health Data, 1993.

In the EU, public expenditure accounts on average for three-quarters of total expenditure. As shown in Table 2.2 the proportion is higher in Luxembourg (91.4 per cent) followed by Belgium, United Kingdom, Spain and Denmark with more than 80 per cent of total expenditure. Portugal has the lowest share of public expenditure with 61.7 per cent while, in the remaining Member States, public expenditures range between 70 and 80 per cent. During the 1980s, the public shares of total health expenditures have decreased in all Member States except in Belgium and Spain. In the latter, the rate of growth was very small (0.25 per cent) compared with a 2 per cent increase during the 1970s. The public share of health expenditure was reduced more markedly in Greece, Ireland and Portugal. The data suggest that, in most countries for which data are available, the majority of public resources are devoted to in-patient care. Denmark and Ireland are shown in the OECD data as allocating over 70 per cent of public health resources to in-patient care,[41] while France, Italy, the Netherlands and the United Kingdom allocate between 50 and 60 per cent. But Belgium and Luxembourg only devote about a quarter of their public health resources to in-patient care. In half the EU countries this share increased during the 1980s. This was particularly the case in Greece and Portugal. But Spain, Italy and the United Kingdom reduced the share of resources on in-patient care substantially during the same period.

Ambulatory care for hospital out-patients and given by doctors outside hospitals consumed almost half of total expenditure in Luxembourg, over 30 per cent in Belgium and Portugal, while in Spain, Ireland and the United Kingdom, it was less than 15 per cent. The share increased significantly in Portugal, Denmark, Ireland and the United Kingdom during the 1980s. Public expenditure on pharmaceuticals varied widely among Member States from over 15 per cent of the total in Germany, Spain, Ireland, Italy and Portugal to under 10 per cent in Greece and the Netherlands and just over 5 per cent in Denmark, but the latter only covers those used in the health insurance scheme. This increased in 9 out of the 12 Member States, particularly in Ireland, Italy, the Netherlands and the United Kingdom.

Provision and utilization
Indicators of the physical volume of inputs also show a striking diversity. As shown in Figure 2.3, the ratio of doctors per 1000 in the population, varies from 4.5 in Italy[42] to 1.4 in Belgium. Germany, Spain, Greece and the United Kingdom are above the average of the European Union of 2.8 doctors per thousand. The ratio of qualified nurses per 1000 population is highest in Belgium (6.5), Denmark (6.4) and Ireland (6.5) which have nearly twice the ratio of nurses of Greece (3.3) and Portugal (2.8). The Southern European Member States have the lowest doctor/nurse ratios with about one nurse per doctor compared with Ireland and the United Kingdom which have more than three nurses per doctor. While ratios of doctor employment in Spain, Greece and Italy are the highest among the European Union, ratios of nurses are among the lowest. The former can be explained by the lack of medical resources planning and by the late introduction of 'numerus clausus' (a limit on the number of medical school places) in these countries. This has led to a high level of doctor unemployment in all three countries.

Figure 2.3: Practising physicians and qualified nurses per 1000 inhabitants, European Union countries, 1989

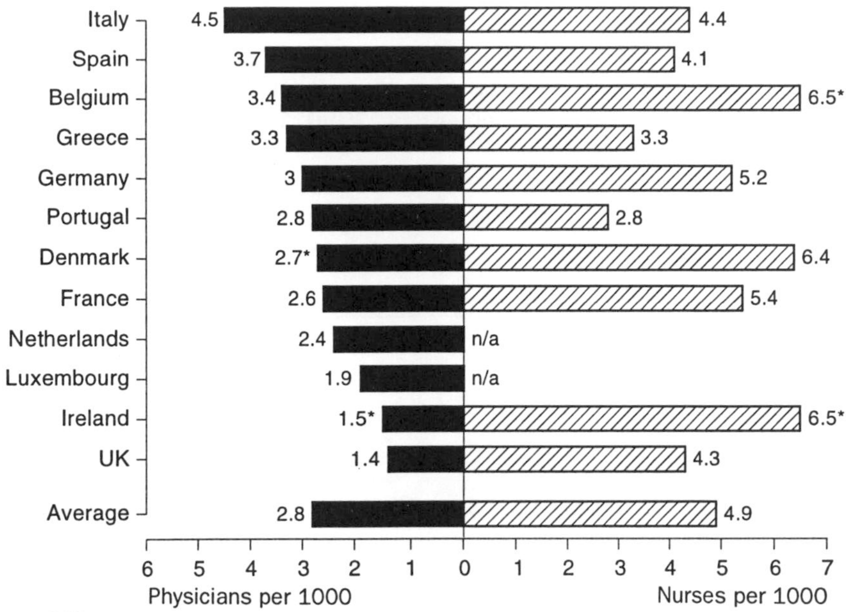

Country	Physicians per 1000	Nurses per 1000
Italy	4.5	4.4
Spain	3.7	4.1
Belgium	3.4	6.5*
Greece	3.3	3.3
Germany	3	5.2
Portugal	2.8	2.8
Denmark	2.7*	6.4
France	2.6	5.4
Netherlands	2.4	n/a
Luxembourg	1.9	n/a
Ireland	1.5*	6.5*
UK	1.4	4.3
Average	2.8	4.9

Physicians per 1000 | Nurses per 1000

* 1988

Note: Source of rate of physicians for Italy from the Federazione Nazionale degli Ordini dei Medici, Rome 1990.

Source: OECD Health Data Version 1.5 (1993).

As shown in Table 2.3, the ratio of hospital beds per thousand inhabitants is highest in Luxembourg (12.3) which has three times the ratio of beds to Spain (4.3). Greece (5.1) and Portugal (4.6), together with Spain, have some of the lowest ratios of in-patient beds per 1000 population. The lower level of bed provision is mainly due to the shortage of chronic or long stay beds in these countries. Denmark, Spain and Portugal have the largest percentage of acute beds. By contrast, the Netherlands with the second highest rate of beds per population has the lowest percentage of acute beds – about 40 per cent of the total. All countries are reducing in-patient beds rates. In those countries for which data on nursing home beds is available there has been a clear increase in the number of beds.

Not surprisingly, there is an association between the provision of beds and the number of bed days per head of population. Luxembourg and the Netherlands use about twice the number of bed days compared with Italy and over three times more than Portugal and Spain. However, there is not a clear relationship between the number of beds and admission rates. Germany, Denmark and France have the highest rates of admission to hospital – all over 20 per 100 population. Next come Belgium and Luxembourg, with over 18 per 100, followed by Ireland and Italy with 14-16 per 100. Then come Greece with 13.1 per 100 and the Netherlands with only 11, but the latter has a very large nursing home sector. The lowest hospital admission rates are found in Portugal (11.2) and Spain (9.8).

**Table 2.3: Indicators of provision and
utilization of in-patient resources (total)
European Union countries, 1990, 1992**

Country	In-patient care beds per 1000 (1990)	In-patient days per head (1992)	In-patient admissions per 100 (1992)
Luxembourg	11.8	3.7	19.9*
Netherlands	11.5	3.8	11
Germany	10.4	3.2	21.3
France	9.7	2.8	23.7
Belgium	9.8	2.4	19.2
Italy	7.1	1.8	15.5*
United Kingdom	5.9	1.9	19.4
Ireland	5.7	2.7	14.5
Denmark	5.6	1.5	21.4
Greece	5.1	1.3	13.1+
Portugal	4.6	1.1	11.2
Spain	4.3	1.1	9.8
EU average	7.8	2.4	16.2

* 1990 + 1991

Source: OECD Health Data and unpublished data from OECD.

Activity indicators also show sizeable variations across the Union, again often with no obvious pattern (see Table 2.4). In ambulatory care the highest rates of visits to doctors are in Germany and Italy – 11 or over per head per year. Then come Belgium and France with over 7 visits per year followed by Spain with over 6. Denmark, the Netherlands and the United Kingdom have between 5 and 6. The rate in Portugal is as low as 2.8 per year. The number of drugs consumed per head is usually up to 50 per cent higher than the rate of visits, but in Italy it is nearly double the rate. France and Portugal stand out as exceptions: in both these Member States, the average visit seems to generate over five drugs. However, the ways in which data are collected and variations in the definitions used raise important issues of comparability.

Table 2.4: Utilization of services in 1989

Country	Home and office visits per head	Consumption of medicines per head
Belgium	7.6	9.3
Germany	11.5**	12.2**
Denmark	5.6	6.1
Spain	6.2	n/a
France	7.2	38
Greece	n/a	21
Ireland	6.6*	9.9
Italy	11*	20.1
Luxembourg	n/a	n/a
Netherlands	5.5	8
Portugal	2.8	16.5
United Kingdom	5.7	7.5

* 1988
** 1987
*** 1986

Source: OECD Health Data.

The public's perception of their health services

Increasing expectations are widely held to be a driving force behind calls for increased health expenditure. The extent to which the public's expectations are met are summarized in Table 2.5. The findings are from a Eurobarometer survey conducted in Member States in 1992.

In the Southern Member States, a minority of people think their health services are of good quality. This is the case with about a quarter of the population in Greece, about a third in Spain and Italy and 43 per cent in Portugal. Major reform is planned in three of these Member States (see the section on major health care reforms in

Chapter 3). In all these Member States, health services are also thought by the majority to be inefficient: this is also the case in Ireland. In most Member States, the majority of the population expect health services to be less good in future because of rising costs. But only a quarter of the population expected this in Luxembourg, 39 per cent in Spain and just under half in France and Greece.

Table 2.5: Public opinion survey on health services in 1992

Country	Quality good*	Services inefficient**	Less good in future+	Willing to pay more++	Only essential services^
Belgium	92	37	54	47	33
Germany	91	27	53	32	22
Denmark	93	46	67	54	26
Spain	36	72	39	51	22
France	95	36	49	38	35
Greece	25	82	47	65	37
Ireland	74	58	65	37	37
Italy	34	82	55	52	33
Luxembourg	89	32	27	61	22
Netherlands	93	32	57	45	26
Portugal	43	80	55	66	45
UK	81	43	64	54	17
EU (12)	71	50	53	45	27

*   'In general do you think that the quality of the health care people receive is good?'

** 'Health services available to the average citizen are inefficient and patients are not treated as well as they should be.'

\+   'In the future the health care provided to the average citizen of this country will be less good because of rising costs.'

++ 'I am willing to pay more for health care benefits even if this means increased taxes.'

^   'The government should provide everyone with only essential health services such as care for serious diseases and encourage people to provide for themselves in other respects.'

Source: Ferrera, M., *EC Citizens and Social Protection: main results from a Eurobarometer survey,* Commission of the European Communities, Brussels, 1993.

A majority of the population willing to pay more in higher taxes for health services was to be found in seven Member States: this was the view of about two-thirds of the population in Greece and Portugal, 61 per cent in Luxembourg but only a small majority in Denmark, Spain, Italy and the United Kingdom. The idea of confining health services only to essential services, such as serious diseases, and encouraging people to make their own provision in other respects did not win the support of the majority in any Member State. The only country where nearly half of the population agreed with this approach was Portugal.

Summary

Overall, this chapter has illustrated the enormous differences in the way that Member States organize, provide and use health care, if the data are successful in comparing like with like. The data do not permit recommendations about appropriate levels of expenditure, provision or utilization. The indicators available are mainly of inputs or intermediate outputs. Apart from the definitional and measurement problems, which reduce their comparability, these indicators say very little about the effectiveness and final outcomes of different patterns of provision or utilization. More doctors, beds or utilization compared with the average says little about their effectiveness. The variation does, however, suggest that there are many different ways of achieving the same objective. Roemer argues that the study of other health systems provides new perspectives from which to view our own and thus learn lessons from others.[43] It is likely that some approaches to the delivery of health care are more effective than others and there is an enormous scope for comparative evaluative studies that make use of the natural laboratory for health and social policy that the Union represents.

3

Cost Containment and Health Care Reforms

All Member States have been taking measures to control the cost of health care, but only to a limited extent in Greece. There is, moreover, considerable convergence in the policies adopted. The methods employed by Member States differ according to the way in which their health care systems are organized and financed. Where the government or the main health insurers own their health care facilities and pay health professionals on a salaried basis – what the International Labour Organization calls the direct system of financing – control is easier than where health care providers are contracted by the government or the main insurers – the indirect system of financing. This chapter provides an overview of the main cost containment measures[44] adopted by different Member States, discusses their effectiveness and shows the potential for further action.

Cost containment measures can operate on consumer demand or on supply. The most common measures acting on consumer demand are described here as cost-sharing. Two further measures to restrict demand for publicly financed services are a no claim bonus (in an insurance scheme) and the introduction of income tax concessions for those who decide to use private services. Another approach is to reduce demand for health services by introducing more promotive and preventive action. The latter will be reviewed in Chapter 7 describing current policies on preventive interventions and health promotion in the Member States. Cost containment measures acting on supply include introducing expenditure ceilings through prospective budgets, sometimes reinforced by controls on manpower, adopting less costly alternatives to in-patient care, influencing authorizing behaviour, reducing the production of doctors and hospital beds, limiting the use of technologies and controlling pharmaceutical prices. These measures aim to contain expenditure through simply reducing costly services, providing incentives to adopt more cost-effective treatments or both.

Cost-sharing

Current health expenditure depends partly on the quantity supplied and partly on the price of the goods or the manpower (salaries or fees) used to supply it. Costs can be contained by operating on either. It also depends on whether particular costs fall on the insurance system or health service or on the patient.

All Member States have, at some stage, used cost-sharing to reduce demand to some extent, but it has not been by any means the most important mechanism for cost containment. It is not possible to make meaningful comparisons of the revenue from cost-sharing between Member States because schemes vary in the extent to which different benefits are provided, such as dentistry, spectacles and the financing of transport costs. Nor has the extent of cost-sharing continuously been increased. In all Member States the issue is a matter of heated controversy between the political parties, probably because of its visibility. Thus cost-sharing may be strengthened at a time when the economic situation deteriorates and then reduced when economic prospects improve. Or the extent of cost-sharing may depend on which political party is in the ascendant at any particular time. But the role which cost-sharing has actually played when compared with total health expenditure has been modest in all the countries studied except Portugal and France. Portugal is planning to vary the level of cost-sharing by income group. In France, cost-sharing amounts to nearly 20 per cent of health expenditure: there has always been a greater role for the 'ticket modérateur' throughout the 50 year history of the French health insurance scheme. However, about 80 per cent of the population have private insurance which pays, in whole or part, the share of cost falling on the patient, so again the impact is small.

Some convergence can also be seen in the fields chosen for cost-sharing. All countries, except Ireland for low income patients, use it for drugs. The extent of co-payment is shown in Table 3.1. There are exemptions for those with low incomes and other categories which vary between Member States.

The proportion of the cost paid by the patient varies by type of drug in Denmark, France, Greece, Italy and Portugal and for certain classes of drug in Belgium. In Germany, it now varies according to pack size. It is flat rate in the United Kingdom and for some drugs in Belgium and a standard proportion of the cost in Spain. In Italy there is a flat rate payment and, in addition, a proportion of the cost is charged to patients. There are extensive exemptions in Belgium, Germany, Denmark, Spain, Italy and the United Kingdom.

There has also been a trend to extend charges for dentistry, at least for adults, where this has been extensively provided in the past, and to reduce or remove subsidies for spectacles, again for adults, except in the case of those with very bad sight. The main variations are in whether countries have charges for visits to doctors and for in-patients.

Exclusion from the coverage of health insurance can be viewed either as a restriction of supply or as a system of 100 per cent cost-sharing. In Germany, certain not medically necessary protheses (e.g. bridges) are no longer reimbursed nor are spectacles for adults, with some exceptions, in the Netherlands and the United Kingdom. The range of items not covered or attracting co-payments has expanded considerably in the Netherlands in 1994, reflecting the view that the public should normally meet part of the cost of health care to promote an awareness of the resources used. These measures have, however, attracted considerable criticism from representatives of the chronic sick.[45] Dentistry is only partially paid for in Denmark for those over 18 years of age.

Table 3.1: General methods of controlling pharmaceutical expenditures in the European Union

Country	List		Patient co-payment system	% Met* by patient
	Positive	Negative		
Belgium	Yes	No	0/25/50/60/75/85/100 % of price plus flat rate	29
Germany	No but from 1996	Yes	flat rate depending on package size	7
Denmark	Yes	No	0/25/50/100% of price	47
Spain	No	Yes	0/40% of price**	32
France	Yes	No	0/40/65/100% of price	34
Greece	Yes	Yes	0/10/25% of price	25
Ireland	No	Yes	0 or up to £90 a month***	n/a
Italy	Yes	No	flat rate plus 40/50% of price	18
Luxembourg	No	Yes	20% of price	n/a
Netherlands	Yes	No	flat rate	8
Portugal	Yes	No	0/30/70% of price	23
UK	No	Yes	flat rate	24

Notes: * The percentages are calculated as in BEUC (1989), based on a sample of 125 drugs.** Patients who are chronically ill have to pay 10 per cent up to a maximum of 400 pesetas per prescription.*** Only for those outside the General Medical Services scheme. Families buying products over £90 of value per month are refunded the excess amount.

Source: Authors' estimates (Abel-Smith and Mossialos (1994)), & BEUC, *Drug prices and drug legislation in Europe*, 1989.

Positive and negative lists for drugs have been introduced in more Member States. The position in this respect is shown in Table 3.1. Ireland extended its negative list of drugs which can be provided for General Medical Services patients in 1982 and is planning a positive list. Germany also removed certain minor drugs from coverage by health insurance in 1983 and more in 1991. It is currently developing a positive list. In 1985, the United Kingdom removed from the National Health Service a range of drugs – mainly those obtainable without prescription – and extended the list in 1992. In 1993, Spain removed 800 drugs from its list. From 1993, non-allopathic drugs were no longer reimbursed in the Netherlands. The negative lists established in Luxembourg and Ireland have not been changed since. Positive lists of what may be paid for are to be found in Belgium, Denmark, France, Italy, the Netherlands, Portugal and Greece but the last is not effectively enforced. There is no positive list in Spain but one is planned.

The number of brand-named products on the market is shown in Table 3.2. It is notable that Norway manages with only about 2000 brand-named products compared to over 23 000 in Germany and 43 000 in the United States.

Table 3.2: The number of drug products on the market

Country	Active ingredients	Brands
Belgium	4150	8906
Germany	8862	23529*
Denmark	2300	4861
Spain	5400	9500
France	4200	8500
Italy	4210	8906
Netherlands	2200	7924
Portugal	4370	12301
United Kingdom	–	10000
Norway	1100	2216
United States	19000	60000**

* Products in the 'Rote' list. It is estimated that the number of products on the market is about 70 000.

** US products in the international market. The national market has 43 000.

Source: Farmindustria, *Indicatori Farmaceutici*, Farmindustria, Rome, 1992.

Expenditure ceilings

The most commonly used method of control is a budget ceiling for all expenditure or large parts of it, reinforced by manpower controls in the case of Spain, Ireland and Italy. Overall budget financing can be applied irrespective of the share of resources collected in compulsory health insurance contributions. Eight Member States have used ceilings of expenditure, normally stated in advance in cash terms, as the main weapon to control costs. In Denmark there are negotiated limits for expenditure by local government. The other seven with capped budgets are Belgium, Germany, Ireland, Italy, Spain, Portugal and the United Kingdom. Belgium and Germany have separate budgets for the main expenditure components but in the latter, health promotion and certain care outside hospital is not budget-limited.

In theory it may seem that non-governmental health insurers cannot be bound by this sort of restriction, but in practice governments have used their powers to restrict or veto any increases in compulsory health insurance contributions, approve any charges levied on patients, and impose reductions in the scope of the insurance offered. Budgets have been imposed on or negotiated within individual hospitals irrespective of their ownership, even where they receive their income from many different health insurers per day of care. This has been done in Germany, the Netherlands and in Belgium where bed-day quotas have the same impact. In Luxembourg, from 1995, overall budgets are to be negotiated for each hospital. In France, this approach has been applied to public hospitals and to operating theatre costs in private hospitals. Private hospitals have also to agree their expected volume of services in advance. In Belgium, the amount of clinical pathology services per day of hospital care is also limited. Thus hospitals in eleven of the twelve countries are or will be under some type of budgetary control. The only exception is Greece which has been trying to upgrade its hospitals and has, until recently, not tried to apply strict control on hospital expenditure.

Budgets have also been applied to total payments to doctors, as in Germany. An increase in services leads to a proportionate reduction in the level of the fees paid. This system was also tried in the Netherlands for specialists but was unsuccessful. A ceiling has been placed on payments for pathology services outside hospital in Belgium and France and, in the latter, also for ambulance services, private practice nurses and other health professionals except doctors. Such systems of control are not needed where doctors are paid salaries. Several Member States use budgets to control out-of-hospital prescribing costs. The main impact of budget control has been on hospitals, leading to pressure to reduce lengths of stay, rationalize the stock, transfer hospitals to other uses or sell them and to develop alternatives to care in hospital.

Limiting doctors and hospital beds

A common theme has been controls on entry to medical education (now exercised in all countries except Belgium and Luxembourg which has no medical school). Of more immediate effect are the controls to enter insurance practice mentioned earlier. In most Member States new capital developments in the public sector, (and in some cases in the private sector as well) have to be authorized by national, regional or local planning bodies. In Belgium, Ireland and the United Kingdom, there has been very extensive firm action to close hospitals or change them to other uses. There are now plans to close 22 000 public hospitals beds in France and 3800 in the Netherlands. In Denmark, also the number of hospitals has been falling, mainly through the closure of small units: further reductions are expected. In Spain, smaller acute hospitals have been transferred to use by the chronic sick or by convalescent patients and some have been closed. It is recognized in Luxembourg that there is a surplus of acute beds, but the procedures to change them for other uses are slow and cumbersome. By contrast, in Portugal, there is still a trend to build more public hospitals with a slight increase in acute beds.

Optimizing the use of technologies

Convergence can also be seen in attempts to control expensive medical equipment by, for example, the health maps used in Belgium, France and Luxembourg. Some attempts elsewhere have been unsuccessful because of exclusion of the private sector. France has recently extended control to cover expensive medical techniques.

A more fundamental approach is to ensure that in the future only those new technologies which are proven to be effective in improving the outcome of treatment are accepted. There has been a growing interest in establishing bodies to undertake technology assessment. It is now estimated that each year, hundreds – perhaps thousands – of new technologies enter the medical care system.[46] The economic burden of technology, together with issues of safety, ethics and social impact, suggest that careful evaluation of technologies is needed before their widespread diffusion into clinical practice, followed by constant subsequent monitoring of their performance. Chapter 4 focuses on these issues and describes the results of a survey of technology assessment activities in the Member States.

Alternatives to in-patient care

Day hospitals and day surgery are well developed in Denmark, Ireland and the United Kingdom and are increasing rapidly in the Netherlands. In contrast, there is very little day surgery in Greece, Spain or Portugal though new hospitals in Portugal are making provision for it. It exists in Belgium, France and Italy on a small scale and an expansion is planned in Luxembourg. Germany has recently sought to encourage it by amending the payment system for doctors.

In nearly all Member States provision of nursing homes and homes for the elderly is under a separate budget from local government or social security, or is left largely to the private sector. The elderly person often has to pay more for care in an old age home than a hospital and it can be very expensive if the private sector is used without any subsidy. In the Netherlands, care in nursing homes is financed under a national insurance scheme and care in homes for the elderly is financed out of the national budget. Only in Ireland and, within the UK, in Northern Ireland does the same budget pay for health care and for old age homes but provision is poorly coordinated with the hospitals. Nursing home care appears to be most fully developed in the Netherlands where there are more occupied beds in nursing homes than in hospitals. Many countries are recognizing the need to make more provision for the elderly by the increasing provision in specialized units. It has been estimated in Germany that 17 per cent of hospital patients do not need care in a hospital and insurance for long term care is being actively discussed. Following an experiment in one county in Denmark, municipalities in some counties now have to pay the county which provides the hospitals for each day any patient had to stay in hospital while waiting for a place in a nursing home. This had the immediate effect of forcing the municipalities to make further provision.

Home nursing is poorly developed in Belgium, Germany, France and Luxembourg where there are plans to develop it; virtually non-existent in Greece and low but growing in Spain, Portugal and Italy (except in the north where it has been better developed). It is provided in the Netherlands by the Cross Societies under a National Insurance scheme. Provision is by the Health Boards in Ireland but on a limited scale and poorly coordinated with the hospital services; there is, in addition, a large private sector. While more extensive in the United Kingdom it is not well coordinated with the hospitals. The most extensive and dynamic service appears to be provided in Denmark where home nurses with cars are available to visit patients, even during the night in most municipalities, for injections and supervision. Data are lacking to make quantitative comparisons of the extent of home nursing.

Influencing the resource use authorized by doctors

Attempts can be made to influence the authorizing behaviour of doctors and dentists. One way of attempting to influence this is by changing the method by which doctors are paid. In 1989, Ireland introduced a change from payment per item of service to capitation payment for primary care doctors under the General Medical Services. Doctors can be faced with changed incentives by altering the relative value scale under fee-for-service systems of payment. Doctors have been paid relatively less for diagnostic tests in France and Germany with the aim of reducing supplier-induced demand. Germany is planning to replace fee-for-service payments with capitation payments plus 'complex service' payments. Per case payments for hospitals are also being gradually introduced. A committee chaired by the Prime Minister in the Netherlands has recently recommended that instead of fee-for-service payments, specialists should receive a basic salary with extra payments for special items of work determined by local agreements. The report coincided with proposals made by the Central Office for Tariffs (COTG) for drastic reductions in the level of fees, based on income data provided for the first time by the various specialist organizations.

The authorizing behaviour of all doctors outside hospital is monitored in Belgium, France and Germany and of all specialists in the Netherlands. Prescribing is examined in most Member States. High authorizers may be warned, threatened or subjected to financial penalties.

France has recently started a system of 'medical references'. These references will be used to assess medical practice outside hospitals. They specify when and how to use different procedures, medical examinations or tests or drug prescriptions related to a disease or health condition. Doctors who do not follow these references could be penalized financially or excluded from the social security system. So far a first batch of 65 references have been developed and accepted by the government.

Other ways of influencing prescribing behaviour are to promote the use of generics or to allow generic substitution: the position on this in Member States is shown in Tables 3.3 and 3.4. These policies have come under sustained attack from the pharmaceutical industry.

Table 3.3: Rights of pharmacists to substitute generics in the EU countries (1993)

Limited form of substitution	With doctor's agreement	In emergencies	None
Spain	Germany	Denmark	France
Italy	Denmark	Luxembourg	Greece
Netherlands	Ireland		
	Portugal		
	Belgium		
	United Kingdom		

Table 3.4: The promotion of the use of generics

Strongly	Yes	No
Germany	Denmark	Belgium
Netherlands	Portugal	Greece
United Kingdom	Ireland	Italy
	Luxembourg	France
	Spain	

Some countries are also seeking to change authorizing behaviour by giving doctors responsibility for budgets, as in the United Kingdom where general practitioners have been authorized to become 'fundholders' or by offering doctors part of any savings as in Ireland. Initial evidence suggests that, contrary to expectations, fundholding has made no difference to referral rates.[47]

From 1993, dentists in the United Kingdom have been paid on a capitation basis for providing most office care to children up to the age of 18. This replaced fee-for-service payments. In the case of patients 18 or over, dentists receive a monthly payment for continuing care and must provide emergency cover, replace restorations which fail within a year and give costed treatment plans. On top of this patients can be charged regulated fees.

Pharmaceutical prices

The position on the control of prices is shown in Table 3.5. All Member States control either the prices or the profits of the pharmaceutical industry, except Germany, Denmark and the Netherlands and partial indirect control in Luxembourg. A newer type of convergence is in the use of a reference price system with the aim of reducing the cost of pharmaceuticals. This operates by grouping similar products and specifying a price which will be fully covered by the insurance, subject to co-payment. Any excess above the reference price has to be paid by the insured person. This system was initiated by Germany in the Union and now applies to about half pharmaceutical expenditure and will be extended still further. It was introduced in the Netherlands in 1991 and Denmark in 1993 and there are powers to introduce it in Luxembourg. It was proposed in Greece but not implemented.

Table 3.5: Outline of systems for curtailing the reimbursement cost of pharmaceuticals in EU countries

Controls	Bel	Ger	Den	Spa	Fra	Gre	Ire	Ita	Lux	Net	Por	UK
Price	X			X	X	X	X	X	X		X	
Profit												X
Reference price	X	X							X			
Price approval before marketing	X			X		X		X			X	
Price approval for reimbursement	X			X	X	X		X			X	

The effectiveness of cost containment measures – potential for further action

The overall effectiveness of cost containment policies is reflected in the health care expenditure trends of the Member States described in the previous chapter (see Figure 2.2). Evidence can be found from particular Member States of the effectiveness of particular measures which were taken. Controls by budget, targets and manpower limits can clearly be made to work. Budgets for hospitals have accelerated reductions in length of stay and budgets for doctors' earnings in Germany have reduced them. Increases in cost-sharing can reduce demand, although, if relatively high, as in France, supplementary insurance may develop, thus negating some of the effects on demand and increasing total expenditure. Changes in the relative value scale in Belgium finally stabilized expenditure on diagnostic tests as have expenditure ceilings in France and Germany. It is often difficult to distinguish the quantitative effect of particular measures because of other changes happening at the same time. There was, for example, a fall in the expenditure of sickness funds on pharmaceuticals of 20.6 per cent on the introduction of the first stage of the reference price system in Germany but the prices of products not under the system increased. The examination of profiles of doctors' work and prescriptions only seems to have limited effect but this may depend on what sanctions are applied and how often they are used.

The obvious way ahead is for Member States which have not yet done so to consider introducing those measures which have proved effective in other Member States. It is clear that some types of action, such as budget controls, are effective if they are rigorously enforced, and in some cases backed up by manpower controls. Cost-sharing can transfer costs from the public sector to the private sector and restrain some costs in total, providing this is not counteracted by extensive private insurance of these co-payments. If such insurance was forbidden or discouraged by the removal of any tax concessions, cost-sharing measures would be more uniformly effective in achieving their objectives. But if they were substantial or if attempts to restrict the effects on the poor are not very effective, de-insuring in this way can have damaging effects on equity and increase inequalities in access to health care.

More Member States could encourage generic prescribing in a variety of ways and more could have positive lists. It is notable that most of the countries without the latter are major exporters of drugs and, presumably, fear repercussions on their exports. Some Member States have hesitated to go far in rationalizing their hospital stock or adopting effective ways of limiting the proliferation of expensive medical equipment, outside as well as inside hospitals. Only preliminary steps have so far been taken in making a reality of a single market for drugs. This should lower the prices of drugs in some Member States and probably increase them in others.

In some Member States, costs could be saved by increasing the number of general practitioners at the expense of specialists and establishing a pattern of referral, as specialists are more likely to use expensive specialized services when it is not strictly necessary. Germany has taken steps to go down this road. Moreover, it is increasingly accepted that an excess of doctors in health insurance practice leads to an excess of costs. The Union has established free movement of doctors but this creates problems for Member States who are trying to limit the number of practising doctors. This is particularly the case in Luxembourg where Belgian trained doctors can so easily practise. This raises the question of whether the Community should follow its free movement directive by limits on the output of doctors in Member States, although this has implications for migration into the Union.

At present, sufficient information is lacking on the long term effects of many of the actions taken by some Member States. An obvious role for the Union is to fill this information gap, in so far as this is possible. The difficulty is that a measure taken in one Member State is often quickly followed by another before there is time to see the long term effects of the first measure.

Major health care reforms

In the last decade health care reforms have been under discussion or introduced in many European Union countries. These reforms aim to contain costs and increase efficiency through more cost-effective patterns of delivery. The general trend of these reforms is towards the introduction of a number of organizational changes intended to promote a greater role for the private sector and a new culture of entrepreneurship and competition among health care providers as well as an overall management decentralization. This section provides an outline of these reforms in five Member States: Spain, Italy, the Netherlands, Portugal and the United Kingdom.

Spain

A parliamentary commission chaired by a former Vice-President reported in 1991. The Abril Report envisaged that the health services would continue to be financed mainly by taxation but the report did not favour a reduction in the role of social security contributions in the financing. It is also argued that charges for drugs and hospital emergency services should be increased to control trivial demand with arrangements to protect the poor. Additional revenue would also be obtained from hotel services and training activities.

As regards the financial arrangements within the service, the report is based to a considerable extent on the British reform but also has important differences. The main similarity is that health areas, broadly corresponding to the British districts, are to contract services from the public and private sectors. Their role is to be purchasers rather than providers, buying on the basis of price, quality and patient satisfaction. But in Spain this would be applied to primary care as well as secondary care. Moreover all the public health units contracted would become autonomous public enterprises. While conditions of service for existing staff would remain with some modification, there would be complete freedom for the health areas to pay new staff on a different basis. Any profit earned from contracts could be given as extra remuneration to staff.

The report envisaged a clear definition of basic services and a need for an explicit decision to add any further services. Every new technology would be assessed for its technical and economic efficiency. If a decision to include the new services were not taken, these extra services would have to be paid for by patients. It is envisaged that for all services patients would be given statements showing the costs.

Although the Abril Report was not explicitly accepted by the government, some of the underlying ideas, such as linking activity with resource allocation, were adopted from 1992 by the main health care agency, INSALUD. But the public hospitals have not been made autonomous. From 1993, following the report, Catalonia and the Basque Country have already been taking some of the steps to create competition (a provider market):

- by separating the purchasing and provision of hospital care,
- by trying to improve management and the information system in the public sector,
- by giving more autonomy to the hospitals and the primary health care centres,
- by trying to introduce more flexible performance-related contracts for health service employees.

Italy

A reform of the Italian National Health Service was finally approved by the government in November 1993. The Service will continue to offer universal coverage financed by social insurance contributions and taxation and most hospitals and primary care centres will remain in public ownership. The aim is to develop incentives for greater efficiency at both the regional and local levels.

The number of local health units (LHUs) will be reduced from 650 to 200-300 so as to serve populations of 100 000 to 250 000. General managers appointed by the Regions will run the new self-governing hospitals and replace the elected committees which currently run LHUs. After a three year transition period, finance both for capital expenditure and current expenditure will be distributed to the 21 regions on a capitation basis adjusted for cross-regional boundary flows. In future, regions will have to keep within their budgets or make up any deficits from their own resources – from local taxes. The regions will distribute funds to the local health units.

All teaching hospitals will become self-governing and other public hospitals providing specialized services and attracting a substantial number of patients from other regions can also apply to become self-governing. They will be funded by their region (instead of the local health unit) partly on an historical basis and partly on a fee structure determined by the region. But these hospitals will also be allowed to sell services on a full cost basis for a limited share of their activity. The regions will specify the fees for the payment of contracted private hospitals: these hospitals may be allowed to make extra charges to patients.

From 1995, patients were to be allowed to opt out of the NHS. They could contract with other insurers run by companies or professional or voluntary associations, who would contract services on behalf of their members in order to achieve higher value for money. These insurers would be allowed to receive their members' share of the per capita-based funds. This proposal was later withdrawn.

The new system is expected to increase efficiency. It will also hold down public health expenditure, while increasing total health expenditure because of the larger role of private payments. The reform has only been partly implemented and the Government elected in the middle of 1994 is unlikely to take the reform any further.

The Netherlands
In 1987, the Dekker Committee reported to the Dutch Government. The committee recommended that the whole population should be compulsorily insured for basic health and social care which excluded drugs, dental care for adults, cosmetic surgery and abortion. Social care was included to secure better integration of health and social care. It aimed to introduce competition both in the insurance market and in the provider market. Three-quarters of the cost of the basic insurance was, under the original plan, to be paid for by income-related contributions paid into a central fund and, on average, a quarter by flat-rate contributions paid to an insurer chosen by the insured person. The flat rate could vary between insurer according to the efficiency of the insurer's purchasing of services, but all persons covered would pay at the same rate and the insurer would be required to accept all applicants. The insurer would make contracts with the providers it chose on the basis of price and quality. Supplementary insurance would be voluntary but again the insurer would be required to accept all applicants. Government regulation would still be required to protect quality, control cost, secure equity and prevent the abuse of monopoly power. It was later decided to enlarge the basic insurance to cover 90-95 per cent of total health care expenditures and to reduce the flat rate contribution from 25 per cent of cost to 15 per cent. Full implementation was planned for 1995.

The government decided to move towards this reform in stages by extending step by step the coverage of the existing universal scheme which already covered care for chronic sickness and disability. Psychiatric care, artificial limbs and appliances were added in 1989, and out of hospital prescribed drugs from 1992. It was intended at first to cover general practice at this stage, but the plan to do so was withdrawn when it encountered political opposition. Each further stage in the reform will have to be approved by parliament. Further progress on these reforms now seems unlikely, following the publication of a critical all-party report which has highlighted the inability to reach agreement on policy.[48]

Portugal
The Portuguese reform aims to improve satisfaction both of consumers and professionals with the services provided by the government and respond to the percep-

tion that higher quality services are provided in the private sector, particularly in high technology services and primary care. It is also an attempt to reduce the centralization of the control of the services and respond to inadequate public funding. A particular problem is the increasing use of hospital emergency rooms instead of the primary care services.

A law passed in 1990 sought to encourage the development of private services, provided that they were licensed and inspected by the government. It allowed higher user charges, but provided that the poor and those with high health risk were exempt. It allowed the development of private services in public hospitals.

A further law of January 1993 decentralized control to five health regions which were allowed to determine user charges subject to minima and maxima laid down by the Ministry of Health, but a further law in August 1993 counteracted this and restored the control of user charges to the Ministry of Health. In addition, the January 1993 law allowed whole-time salaried doctors to engage in private practice, provided they continued to give the same time to the National Health Service.

The law of January 1993 also provided for public services to be managed or provided under contract by other organizations (public or private). These organizations could include local authorities, religious organizations or social insurance funds. Alternatively contracts could be made with groups of doctors who would be paid for providing services by the Regional Health Authorities and were to be allowed to charge others for the services they provided. In addition, Regional Health Authorities could make contracts with private doctors.

A further provision in the law of January 1993 encouraged patients to transfer to private insurers who will cover all their defined health care needs. In return, these private insurers will receive from the government for each insured person less than the average cost per head of the National Health Service. The insurers will decide how they pay providers: it is hoped that this will lead to group practices being formed to provide out of hospital care. Discussions are in progress with private insurers to see if they can provide full health care at acceptable prices. It is not intended that the premia will be community-rated but, once an insured person is accepted, the insurer will have to continue to provide services throughout the life of that insured person, if the insured person wishes it.

The United Kingdom
The United Kingdom has, from 1991, used a system of a provider market with the aim of increasing efficiency and thus enabling health needs to be met within a lower total of expenditure. The District Health Authorities purchase hospital services from public and private hospitals under contracts placed on the basis of cost and quality. Parallel to this, groups of general practitioners covering about a third of patients have been allowed to opt to become purchasers of services. They buy, with their budgets, out-patient consultations and diagnostic tests, a limited number of elective acute hospital in-patient services and part of community services for their patients, but not emergency and obstetric services. Hospitals have increas-

ingly been allowed to become 'trusts', which gives them considerable freedom from the regulations governing the National Health Service, particularly in determining the levels of pay of their staff. About 90 per cent of expenditure is made by hospitals with this status. It is too early to assess the effects of these reforms but there is evidence that fundholding general practitioners are obtaining better services from hospitals although this is probably due, at least in part, to their receipt of considerably greater financial resources than non-fundholding practices, with fundholders getting about one third more money per patient.[49]

In London, districts are contracting with local hospitals rather than the more expensive central teaching hospitals. Some of the latter are amalgamating as a preliminary to reducing beds, although this is being done within a planned rather than a market context. There is also evidence that the transaction costs of the system have increased. There is some evidence of increased hospital activity but this is subject to major problems of definition and much may be artificial.[50]

Since 1974, the National Health Service has been run in England by 14 planning Regional Authorities and under them originally 193 District Health Authorities which provided the hospital and community services. Parallel to the district authorities were Family Health Service Authorities responsible for administering the contracts of general practitioners, pharmacists and dentists. In a further change to the system, the Regional Health Authorities are to be abolished from 1996 and the Service is to be run through eight regional offices of the central NHS Executive. The number of District Health Authorities is to be reduced to 108 by April 1994 and 80 to 90 eventually. These Authorities will be enabled to merge with the Family Health Service Authorities. It is expected that these changes will save 1900 administrative jobs.

Evaluation of the reforms
It is too early to see the effects of the reforms. In all the countries described above, except the United Kingdom, reforms have not yet been fully implemented. In the latter, where implementation is furthest advanced, the evidence is still inconclusive and complicated by continuing and frequent further changes. In addition, it is difficult to attribute those changes in process and outcome that have occurred to a particular policy. In theory, provider markets can be expected to yield greater efficiency savings among providers, although in practice these may be outweighed by high transaction costs. Furthermore, markets may increase inequity and encourage the provision of ineffective, if lucrative, interventions. There is certainly growing evidence of high transaction costs and inequity in the reformed United Kingdom system. Nonetheless, if these can be shown to have more beneficial effects than disadvantages, there may be scope for extending them by, for example, giving each insured person a free choice of insurer with the contribution income distributed between insurers on the basis of risk, if suitable means of assessing this can be developed. The problem of predicting risk has defied resolution in the Netherlands reforms and in the British system of fundholding general practitioners and may

actually be impossible. Alternatively, in systems funded from general taxation, health authorities could place contracts with providers, instead of giving them budgets.

There is some evidence of convergence in the way that Member States are reforming their health systems with a general trend towards the public contract model although there are important differences in the ways that this model is being implemented. Several Member States are undergoing similar public debates and face common difficulties in establishing and implementing reforms. A better understanding of the process and effects of introducing a major organizational change such as provider competition in one Member State can help to plan and predict the results of adopting similar patterns in the others. There is then an important role for the Union in monitoring and providing information on the reforms under way in Member States.

4

Outcomes Management and Technology Assessment

During the 1980s a growing body of evidence emerged concerning variations in the rate at which health care interventions were used.[51] These variations are seen at all levels, between countries, between regions, and between individual doctors. Subsequent work has demonstrated that much of the variation is due to clinical uncertainty, partly due to the absence of good evaluative research on which to base decisions. There is also growing recognition that the vast majority of medical interventions have never been evaluated adequately. As a result, there is increasing interest in several Member States in the issue of appropriateness of health care interventions, based on the concept that reductions in ineffective treatment may be a valuable strategy in reducing health care costs without reducing health benefits. This chapter examines the use of information on outcomes to inform the purchasing of health services. It begins with a review of the concept of managing health outcome, continues with an examination of a specific application of outcomes information, needs assessment, and concludes with a review of technology assessment.

Managing health outcome

Managing health outcome is based on research into what works – what is effective in terms of outcome – and what patients choose when given an informed choice. For some conditions, patients may prefer watchful waiting, at least at first, to active intervention. This was found to be the case with 80 per cent of patients with severe prostate symptoms in a study in the United States who were given an informed choice.[52] There are many common conditions for which there are a variety of options. They include angina pectoris, gallstones, cataracts, arthritis of hip or knee and herniated disc. In many of them there are serious options between surgery, medical management and, in not a few cases, watchful waiting.[53] In an age when medicine has become highly specialized with technology-driven sub-specialities and a willingness for insurers to pay for unevaluated technologies, what is supplied may well be far above what can be proved to work or what patients would want if they were fully informed. Compared to any other industry, the health care industry as a whole spends remarkably little on testing its final products or finding out what its final consumers really want. This activity can be carried out by building on existing agencies, creating networks, exchanging knowledge and maximizing co-operation with international organizations.

Thus one aim for the future should be to provide information to enable Member States to restrict unnecessary services. This would include those which are ineffectual, inappropriate, or over-used in the sense that they could be provided less expensively. Inappropriate services include treatments which are too risky in the sense that the probable risk exceeds the probable benefit or using a type of care which is effective for a different condition to the one with which the patient is presenting. Estimates of unnecessary services range from 30 per cent to 60 per cent of health spending in Canada[54] and inappropriate services are estimated to be 30 per cent of health care in the United States. This last estimate probably exaggerates the possible saving, as it has been made by generalization from a select group of procedures to all health care and, while it is often possible to determine that an intervention was inappropriate after it has been administered, it is less easy in advance. Secondly, if some overused procedures were cut back, other types of procedures would take their place. And there is also the problem of underuse which, if this were made good, would reduce the potential savings. But there is still a hidden area where it is not known whether care is effective, appropriate and efficient in the use of resources or not. It is always difficult to estimate the prospective benefits for individual patients.

But it is not just whole services which may be unnecessary. There is also the question of what interventions are a necessary part of giving the service. As has been pointed out:

> Appendectomy is worth funding, at least for a clear-cut diagnosis. The real issue is not whether to perform the appendectomy; it is whether to fund countless marginal interventions that are potentially part of the procedure – marginal blood tests and repeat tests; preventive antibiotic therapy before surgery; the number of nurses in the operating room; the backup support on call or in the hospital. Even more marginal elements will arise during the recovery phase: exactly how many days of hospital stay are permitted, how often the physician should make rounds, how many follow-up tests there should be, and so on. Many of these are predicted to offer more benefits than harm, but with margins so small that one could argue that resources ought to be used elsewhere.[55]

One possible approach to reducing unnecessary services would be the development of medical purchasing guidelines. A systematic review of the impact of guidelines has shown that they can change medical practice and improve patient outcome.[56] Guidelines should be established by a systematic review of existing medical literature to learn what treatments – and what steps within those treatments – are necessary and efficient judged by the outcome. This process should build on the Cochrane collaboration, a group of research centres throughout the world that arose from the United Kingdom Perinatal Epidemiology Unit in Oxford, that co-ordinate systematic reviews of evidence on specific topics. But many new studies will be needed comparing the outcome of different treatment regimes. In many fields, a formal random trial would be considered unethical. But medical customs vary between Member States and it would be possible to see what inputs improve outcomes or make no difference to them. Of course individual cases vary, so do the circumstances in which medical care is delivered: medical care should not operate on precise specifications with no differences between doctors and patients. But there are, nevertheless, unsupportable variations in medical practice. For all these reasons it is difficult to estimate the potential savings. Going down this road would be a major task taking years and involving considerable expenditure. 'Practice guidelines' are used widely in the United States for quality assurance and, increasingly, to guide reimbursement decisions. For example, practice guidelines have been established in the State of Maine for 20 conditions in 4 high risk specialties (obstetrics gynaecology, radiology, emergency medicine and anaesthetics). They were developed by an advisory committee consisting of insurers, doctors and business, labour and consumer groups and approved by the State. The experiment is intended to continue until 1996.[57] The Danish National Board of Health in collaboration with scientific societies, has a programme of developing practice guidelines based on systematic reviews of research-based evidence. As mentioned earlier, the 'medical reference' system has already started to be introduced in France. In the United Kingdom, the Royal Colleges and some specialist associations have been active in developing guidelines. There are also local examples developed in partnership between hospital doctors and general practitioners and, in some areas, they are being used to inform purchasing decisions.

Once guidelines are formulated, the next task would be to get them accepted and supported by health professionals. Further research is needed on the most effective strategies for changing doctors' behaviour, as simply publishing them has not been found to be effective[58] but there is a growing body of literature describing factors associated with success and failure, including the need to ensure that they are developed using explicit methods and are recognized to be scientifically valid.[59] Acceptance is eased if the leading medical organizations are involved closely in setting the guidelines and come to 'own' the results. This would have the additional advantage of getting the national medical organizations to meet each other and begin to develop on a Union-wide basis. This, however, may be complicated by the extent to which national medical organizations see themselves as having a major role in maintaining professional standards, such as the British and Irish Royal Colleges, or function more as a trade union, such as the French Ordre des Médecins. The guidelines would need to be assimilated by providers and, hopefully, incorporated in medical education and promoted through continuing education. A further step would be to use them in what insurers are prepared to reimburse and in judgements of quality when contracts are placed with providers. Information systems would need to be programmed to identify unacceptable breaches in the guidelines, although this would be expensive and, technically, very difficult.

Needs assessment

The focus in some health care reforms on the requirement to ensure that services are appropriate and related to population need has stimulated interest in the concept of needs assessment. This has received most attention in the United Kingdom, largely as a result of the demands of the internal market but work is also in progress in some other Member States such as Spain. The basic principle is that an explicit definition is developed of those in need of treatment (defined as the ability to benefit). This combines research-based evidence on effectiveness with formal consensus development, using expert opinion, where the evidence is conflicting or missing.

Having defined those individuals with a need for treatment, based on information on outcomes at various stages of disease, and developed a survey instrument that can detect them, a survey is then undertaken in a defined population to determine the prevalent need.[60] Interventions which have been examined in this way include hip replacement,[61] cataract extraction[62] and prostatectomy.[63]

The results can then be related to the existing provision of services to determine whether there is over- or under-provision. Typically, it is found that there are individuals in the community who would benefit from treatment but who are not receiving it and others who have received it without benefit.

This approach has several important limitations. It can only be used to examine those interventions for which individuals who would benefit can be defined using a non-invasive survey instrument. Thus, for example, need for cholecystectomy, could not be assessed. It measures prevalent, not incident, need. The level of prevalent need is a function of the incident need (i.e. the level of provision required to meet need) and the duration of the condition. The incident need can be inferred using modelling techniques but this is complex and involves many assumptions.

This process requires the availability of a population-based register containing age from which a representative sample can be drawn. This is unavailable in some Member States. Finally, it must be combined with information on treatment preference as some of those who would benefit from treatment may, nonetheless, not wish to receive it. Despite these limitations, it offers a mechanism to identify under-provision of services and thus to inform decisions about redirecting resources.

Technology assessment

One particular aspect of the issue of effectiveness is the introduction of new and expensive technologies which can be used in such a way that there is no improvement in outcome. A technology can be expensive either because of the cost of the initial equipment which can now be very large[64] or because skilled staff are needed to use it. It is not enough to know that a technology is safe or that it does what it purports to do and does it with accuracy. The vital question is whether it improves outcome and on which patients. An effective new technology can so easily replace an older and much less expensive technology for routine use when, for many conditions, the outcome using the old technology may be just as good as with the new. And it is by no means uncommon for the old technology to continue to be used as well as the new which is proved to give better results. To establish the appropriate and efficient use of a new technology is by no means easy. Considerable resources are needed for this type of research and it cannot be done quickly.

Technology assessment includes the evaluation of technical performance, clinical efficacy, safety, economic efficiency, organizational impact, social consequences, and ethical implications.[65,66,67,68] In all cases, economic evaluation ('comparative analysis of alternative courses of action in terms of both their costs and consequences'[69]) must play a key role.

The most frequent tasks undertaken by organizations involved in technology assessment are:[70]
- monitoring emerging or existing technologies and setting priorities for evaluation;
- ensuring that appropriate research is undertaken;
- systematically reviewing and disseminating information.

The process of selecting technologies for assessment must be designed carefully. In most Member States this is largely an informal process with no systematic procedures involved. An exception is the United Kingdom where a Standing Group on Health Technology exists under the aegis of the NHS Research and Development Programme.[71]

A survey of technology assessment activities under way in the EU Member States is reported below in some detail. It reveals the following general themes.
- Technology assessment research activities are concentrated in half of the Member States. Application of the evidence produced in different contexts is not straightforward, and circulation of information is very limited at present.
- Most technology assessment activities, and almost all primary research programmes, are undertaken by academic or independent institutions. The evidence they produce, however, is seldom made available to decision-makers in a timely and effective fashion.
- Technology assessment activities are extremely dispersed within the most active Member States. Many bodies operate with limited staff and funding, pursuing similar objectives. Few, if any, efforts have been made to co-ordinate research and provide incentives for the concentration of resources on specific projects.

In **Belgium**, the National Commission for Hospital Planning has conducted studies on CT scanners, coronary artery by-pass grafting, and lithotripsy. The reports resulted from wide consultation with practitioners and experts in the country. Other studies have been undertaken by multidisciplinary teams affiliated to academic institutions. The Institute of Hygiene and Epidemiology (IHE), active at regional level, is in charge of the evaluation of safety of health care practices.

Responsibility for technology assessment in **Denmark** is devolved largely to county level although the Committee for Health Technology Evaluation, which is part of the National Board of Health (an advisory body to the Ministry of the Interior, set up in 1982), operates at both central and local levels. It has evaluated at least four technologies in the health care domain, focusing on technical properties, safety, impact on health outcomes and health care organizations. Evaluations are based on reviews of existing evidence and do not usually involve primary research. The Medical Research Council's Committee for Health Services Research and Health Technology Assessment, established in 1981, is involved mainly in co-ordination, support and initiation of research, rather than direct evaluative activities. In 1986, the National Board of Technology was set up as an independent body operating under the supervision of a parliamentary committee. It is aimed at 'following and initiating global assessment of the potential possibilities of technological development and its consequences for society and the individual citizen, and to support and stimulate the public debate on technology'. It has so far evaluated social and ethical concerns related to certain technologies, mainly by means of expert opinions and consensus-building methods. The Danish Hospital Institute, linked to the County Council Association, undertook more than 20 technology assessment studies, evaluating different aspects of the impact of equipment, medical procedures, prevention programmes and organizational models. Evaluations are typically based on existing evidence.

In **France,** a governmental agency (ANDEM – Agence Nationale pour le Développement de l'Evaluation Médicale) was established in 1990 to develop technology assessment in France, although it also undertakes on its own evaluations of equipment, procedures and prevention or health promotion programmes. Studies can be requested by the Minister for Health or any Director of the Ministry. The agency does not undertake or sponsor primary research. Technologies are assessed by means of an explicit method of synthesis of scientific literature and expert opinion, primarily looking at their safety, clinical efficacy and ethical implications. Some 20 technologies have been evaluated so far. ANDEM plays an important role in developing the French practice guidelines mentioned earlier, by validating them and running consensus conferences.

CEDIT (Comité d'Evaluation et de Diffusion des Innovations Technologiques), part of the Assistance Publique – Hôpitaux de Paris hospital network, has undertaken over 100 studies since it was established in 1982. Methods for assessment are based largely on synthesis of information and expert opinions, but primary research is also carried out. Another body undertaking early assessment of health care technology is the Commission Nationale d'Homologation but its assessments are concerned with technical rather than social aspects as it regulates what public hospitals can purchase. The commission is supervised by the Centre National de l'Equipement

Hospitalier (CNEH), an independent body whose role is changing. It assessed a significant number of health care technologies (equipment, procedures and organizational models), by means of syntheses of existing evidence or sponsoring external research. Technology assessment initiatives have also been promoted by the main National Health Insurance Fund (CNAMTS), and the National Institute for Health and Medical Research (INSERM). The latter has recently supported the establishment of a new health economics group to take part in technology assessment activities. Finally, there is a parliamentary office (Office Parlementaire d'Evaluation des Choix Scientifiques et Technologiques), with a limited role in the field of health care. It has undertaken two studies on prevention and health promotion programmes, but no primary research is involved. In spite of all this activity, it has been suggested that 'there is limited knowledge of health care technology assessment in France, particularly among clinical doctors. Until recently, decisions were based primarily on other factors'.[72]

A parliamentary 'Committee for Research, Technology and Technology Assessment' was established in **Germany** in 1985; half of its members are Members of Parliament, half are experts. In 1988 it devolved research responsibilities to the Institute for Applied Systems Analysis (AFAS – Abteilung für Angewandte Systemanalyse), that belongs to the Nuclear Research Centre (Kernforschungszentrum). The Committee retained control of selecting topics, authorizing projects, controlling finances and releasing reports to the public. In this framework, the political majority controls the technology assessment process,[73] although the external research unit maintains scientific independence. The Institute for Applied Systems Analysis has not undertaken research in the field of health care; however, the Parliamentary Office for Technology Assessment (TAB – Technikfolgenabschätzungsbüro Deutscher Bundestag), which is run by AFAS, recently carried out studies on gene therapy and genome analysis. Both were aimed at assessing the social consequences and ethical implications by means of reviews of existing evidence and sponsored research.

Many studies have been undertaken by research institutions (e.g. the Environment and Health Research Centre – GSF, Forschungszentrum für Umwelt und Gesundheit GmbH; the Institute of Sociology, Rehabilitation and Preventive Research of the University of Hamburg – RPF, Institut für Soziologie, Arbeitstelle Rehabilitations- und Präventionsforschung; or the Institute for Systems and Technology Analysis in Biomedicine – SYSTA BIOMED, Institut für System- und Technologieanalysen in der Biomedizin). However, at least one aspect of technology assessment, economic evaluation, seems to have received little attention:[74] 'in the FRG we are far from routine application of the instruments of economic evaluation in support of decision-making processes – efficiency studies must still be considered as individual attempts and efforts'. Partial evaluations (considering only costs and benefits to investors) are undertaken for defining prices for individual medical services.

Technology assessment activities in **Greece** are very limited. Possible reasons include the fact that most medical equipment is imported and imports are largely unregulated; public expenditure on technology is rather low; decision-making on the adoption and diffusion of technology is fairly centralized and evaluations at this level consider only safety; evaluation skills are limited and little funding is available for research.

In **Ireland**, expensive items of equipment are funded directly by the Department of Health. Any request for implementation of equipment has to be supported by specific clinical and economic evaluations, although no formal guidelines have been issued by the Department of Health. National policies on health care technology are also set, particularly for planning access to facilities on a country-wide basis. The extent to which these two forms of assessment are consistent with comprehensive technology assessment models adopted in other countries is unclear. They only take into account variables relevant to the settings in which equipment is to be implemented (estimates of workload, running costs, implications for staffing, etc.).

In **Italy**, the recent reform of the National Health Service is likely to shift technology assessment responsibilities from the centre to the Regions. However, at present there is no governmental or parliamentary body institutionally committed to technology assessment. During the 1980s, the National Research Council (CNR), funded two national research programmes on health care technology. Many hospitals and academic research centres took part. An independent research centre examining biomedical equipment (CRSTBS – Centro Ricerche e Studi sulle Tecnologie Biomediche e Sanitarie) has been established in 1990 in Trieste. Staff include engineers, physicists, and biologists, but the Centre also counts on the contributions from external scientists. It has just completed a research programme, funded by the Ministry of Health, involving technical, clinical and economic assessment of magnetic resonance imaging, lithotripsy, laser scalpels, PACS and laboratory automatic analysers.[75] Technologies were evaluated by means of primary research, although clinical efficacy was assessed by panels of experts on the basis of the evidence available. The Centre has also produced a scenario of health care technology in Italy until 1995, and is currently supervising the acquisition and utilization of equipment in Friuli Venezia Giulia Region on behalf of the Regional Government. An office for technology assessment has been set up by Veneto Region in 1993, but it has not undertaken any activity so far. Instead, academic and independent centres like CeRGAS of Bocconi University in Milan and CRESA in Turin, are very active in the evaluation of social and economic consequences of health care technology.

Given the size and population of the country, problems related to health care technology in **Luxembourg** are quite different from those present in most of the other EU countries. Costly equipment on a special list can be purchased by individual hospitals only when authorized by the Minister for Health. However, assessment is not a necessary condition for granting authorization.

In **The Netherlands**, technology assessment activities began in 1972, when a Working Party on Medical Technology was set up to develop procedures for testing equipment in hospital settings. Its activity was subsequently expanded to cover a large number of hospitals, and a Co-ordination Committee was created. TNO (the National Institute for Applied Scientific Research, funded by the government and by the industry) played a key role in this process. TNO developed a Medical Technology Assessment Programme primarily aimed at assessing the impact of equipment, medical procedures and organizational models on health outcomes, by means of primary research. Some evaluations also cover other aspects of the impact of technology, synthesizing existing evidence. Some 20 technologies have been evaluated so far.

The most important technology assessment centre in the Netherlands is the Health Council, whose role has been defined by law. Evaluations are carried out either internally or by means of groups of experts, appointed for specific studies. Attention to economic and social aspects is relatively recent; the assessment process previously focused on technical and medical issues. Evaluative activity is also undertaken by the Sick Funds Council (Ziekenfondsraad), which has an advisory role with central Government. In the mid 1980s it developed a two-stage strategy for rationalizing the inclusion of health services in benefit packages. The Investigative Medicine programme, started in 1988, represents the latest development of the Council's assessment activities, aimed at funding external prospective research projects. About 40 projects have been sponsored so far, most of which related to new medical interventions; 70 per cent concern therapy and 30 per cent diagnosis.[76] Safety, social consequences, clinical efficacy and cost-effectiveness of technologies are assessed.

The Netherlands Organization for Technological Assessment has been established in 1986 as a body linked to the Ministry of Education and Science, with an advisory role to the parliament. It has not had a significant role in health care technology assessment. At least two academic institutions deserve to be mentioned. First, the Institute for Medical Technology Assessment (IMTA), linked to Erasmus University, which has evaluated some 80 technologies in the health care field. The impact on health outcomes, social consequences and cost or cost-effectiveness are assessed by IMTA, usually undertaking primary research. Second, there is the Department of Clinical Epidemiology and Biostatistics of the Academic Medical Centre (Amsterdam), whose involvement in technology assessment is relatively recent. It undertakes primary research, always assessing efficacy, social and economic consequences. The Netherlands Organization for Quality Assurance in Hospitals (CBO), set up in 1979 by the National Specialists Organization and the Dutch Association of Medical Directors of Hospitals, is involved mainly in assessing established technology, particularly for safety, effectiveness, appropriate use and doctors' acceptance.

The possibility of setting up a national programme for health care technology assessment in **Spain** was considered by the Government within the European Union Convergence Plan. At present, some central regulatory powers, particularly towards industry, are exercised by the Drugs Directorate. Technology assessment programmes exist at local level. The Catalan Office for Health Technology Assessment (Oficina Tècnica d'Avaluació de Tecnologia Mèdica), was established in 1991 within the Department of Health of the Autonomous Region of Catalonia. This agency has so far evaluated some 20 technologies (equipment, procedures and health programmes). Evaluations are primarily concerned with safety, impact on health care organizations, ethical implications and clinical efficacy. Primary research is undertaken or sponsored, but comprehensive literature reviews are also used. Economic evaluations are sometimes carried out, aimed at assessing the cost per life year saved by the technology, or simply its cost per unit of output. The Office is also involved in the process of the purchase of expensive equipment and in defining reimbursement systems for technology.[77] A similar agency (Servicio de Evaluación de Tecnologías Sanitarias) has been set up recently within the Department of Health of the Basque Government.

In the **United Kingdom**, a new Research and Development strategy for the National Health Service was launched in April 1991. The goal is to establish an R&D infrastructure, with a director of R&D and an R&D committee in each regional health authority, aimed at supporting the formulation of policies, management, provision and purchasing of health care, assessment of health care needs, and assessment of outcomes and quality.[78] The Central Research and Development Committee (CRDC) has recently undertaken a broad consultation of organizations involved in research for setting priorities for technology assessment. The Cochrane Collaboration was established as part of the Information Systems Strategy supporting the R&D programme. This provides a mechanism for centres throughout the world systematically to review evidence from randomized controlled trials on medical procedures, equipment, drugs and prevention or health promotion programmes. Another centre, the Centre for Reviews and Dissemination, was recently established by the Government. It is mainly concerned with the impact of technology on health care organizations and health outcomes (the latter assessed on the basis of the existing evidence), but it also undertakes economic evaluations. Some 10 technologies have been assessed so far, and a series of 'Effective Health Care Bulletins' have been published.

Most primary research activities are currently carried out within the universities, and funded by the Department of Health, research councils, health authorities, pharmaceutical and medical equipment industry, or medical research charities. In the late 1980s, assessment activities and consensus conferences have been developed on selected technologies by the King's Fund Centre for Health Services Development.

An Economic and Operational Research Division operates at the Department of Health. It is primarily concerned with promoting rather than undertaking research. Major studies commissioned from independent bodies during the 1980s include heart transplant programmes, care of the elderly and people with learning disabilities. The Scientific and Technical Services Branch (STB) of the Department of Health is in charge of technical appraisal of medical equipment, undertaken at a series of centres in hospitals and medical schools. A Parliamentary Office of Science and Technology (POST) was also established in 1989, linked to a charitable trust fund created with support from MPs, industry, professional associations, and foundations. Its main task is producing monthly 'Briefing Notes' that cover subjects of current political interest. However, technology assessment activities have also been started from 1990, focusing attention on ethical, social and economic consequences. Studies on drinking water standards and technology-push in drugs costs have been undertaken in the health domain by external scientists, largely relying on existing evidence.

Finally, the National Audit Office and the Audit Commission must be mentioned for their evaluative activities, although usually focused more on efficiency than on the effectiveness of interventions. Both have issued reports concerning the use of selected technologies in the NHS, and the former has also produced guidelines for 'Value for money' studies.

This review has highlighted certain features of the existing efforts to evaluate health technology in Europe. First, the process of selection of technologies for assessment needs to be carefully designed. The selection of technologies for assessment in EU countries seems to be largely an informal and discretional process with the exception of the United Kingdom where a series of expert committees have recently produced a report setting out priorities for research.[79] There seem to be no systematic and structured procedures to assist it. In many organizations involved in technology assessment in the United States, priorities are set by special committees on the grounds of explicitly stated criteria such as:
- the impact on aggregate cost of health care (cost-saving or cost-inducing);
- significant variability in medical practices;
- the prevalence of treatable conditions;
- the potential impact on patient outcome (benefit and risk);
- social and ethical concerns;
- the availability of a reliable base of knowledge;
- the probability that the assessment will produce conclusions that can potentially change the use of the technology.

Second, there needs to be more harmonization of evaluative techniques and their orientation toward a common goal. Crucial issues currently on the agenda include:
- improving the evaluation of health outcomes by means of more reliable measures of health state utilities;
- understanding the relation between outputs and outcomes, which is critical in diagnostic and preventive interventions;
- accounting for the distribution of costs and benefits of technology over time (discounting);
- making assessment models more dynamic and flexible for improving transferability and validity in situations characterized by complexity and uncertainty;
- deciding what costs to bring into account and how to measure benefit or utility so as to make studies comparable.

At present, throughout the Community, for only one type of technology is evidence of effectiveness required – drugs. Here the task of establishing it rests with the manufacturer and the indications for its use have to be approved by licensing authorities. There would seem no good reason why the same should not apply to equipment and certain devices. It would not seem an impossible task to define what new technologies were required to go through this process. In the United States, the Food and Drug Administration has to evaluate equipment and devices as well as drugs.

In view of the large number of medical devices and equipment coming on to the market, this is a task which would seem most appropriately coordinated at Union level, though suitable agencies in Member States would be commissioned to give appraisals of the validity of the research quoted by manufacturers. Different systems of evaluation may be appropriate depending on whether the product is for use in, on or completely outside the human body.

While a manufacturer can prove effectiveness in terms of outcome on some use, the problem remains that the practice of using it more widely often develops. Thus there is a need for further research to establish whether there are further applications which lead to improvements in outcome. This type of research would also seem suitable for coordination and finance at the Community level. Moreover, the standardization of the procedures for accepting new technologies between Member States would assist the manufacturers of useful new technologies and secure their more rapid introduction. On the other hand, the detrimental side effects of treatment can be more easily detected when monitoring a larger population.

A further problem is the lack of evaluation of existing technologies. Little is known about the extent to which many of them improve outcome and this is a gap which also needs to be filled. Customary use can so easily be guided more by convenience than proven evidence of effectiveness.

The skills to undertake evaluations and appraise them are not well developed in every Member State. And as shown above, present efforts are scattered and there could well be duplication of effort. If the lead were taken at Community level, this could result in the concentration of effort in a number of carefully chosen centres which could also act as training centres for further research workers entering the field. There are undoubtedly economies of scale in the concentration of effort in this relatively new field. Information needs to be exchanged on planned work to avoid the duplication of effort.

5

Establishing Priorities
in Practice

Historically, decisions on priorities have arisen from an implicit bargain between the medical profession and large purchasers, such as governments. But three trends have emerged as a result of resources being squeezed. Firstly there is a trend towards making decisions on priorities more explicit, open and democratic, especially when they are likely to be controversial, as in the case of limiting or stopping the supply of certain services. In some cases this has resulted in involving the public far more in decisions on priorities, partly to stimulate wider debate and understanding of scarcity in relation to health care funds, partly to give greater legitimacy to difficult political and moral decisions, and partly because no-one knows how best to make these complex decisions, thus involving a plurality of interests is likely to produce more acceptable results.

The second major trend has been to attempt to spend scarce resources more effectively. Apart from stimulating a wave of health sector reforms across Member States, this has also increased interest in developing and using information on the effectiveness of specific treatments. Thirdly, there has been a trend towards examining the ethical issues involved in setting priorities.

Figure 5.1 shows the major factors involved in priority setting. However, the relative influence of each factor on the resulting priorities is far from clear and thus very difficult to quantify. Also their role and relative importance vary widely among Member States and any attempt to co-ordinate policy at the level of the Union must take account of this diversity, in terms both of the priorities that are generated in Member States and of the ability of governments and other bodies to influence them.

The following paragraphs review the roles played by these factors in the Member States, focusing first on the responsibilities for health and health care within government ministries, recognizing the requirement for the Commission to work through governments of Member States. Second, some issues relating to the differ-

ing roles of government, at all levels, and of public sector bodies in establishing
and implementing priorities are explored. Third, the role of the public and of provider groups in Member States is examined. Finally, the use of research-based evidence in priority setting is discussed.

Figure 5.1: Factors involved in setting priorities

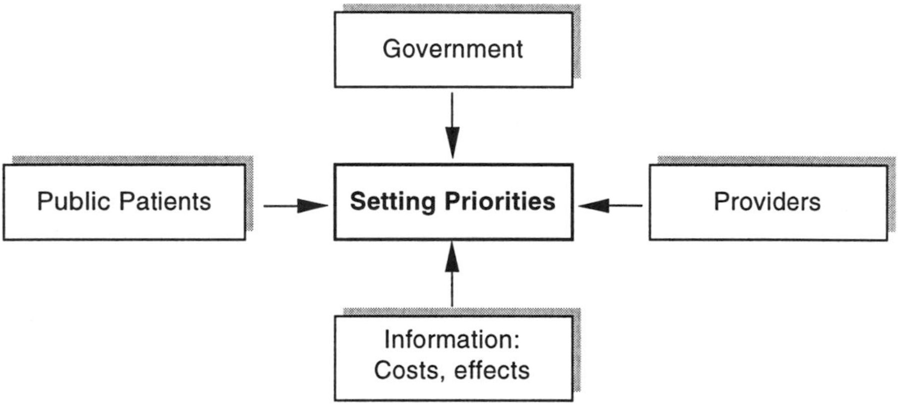

Ministerial responsibilities within central government

The extent of government involvement in establishing priorities varies enormously,
largely reflecting the diversity in the scale and functions of the lead ministry. The
role of government is greatest where health services are funded out of general taxation and in public ownership. In addition, there is variation in the level of government at which these functions are based.

The establishment of health policies is a complex process because of the impact
on health of factors within the competence of many different ministries. Typically,
the lead ministry is that responsible for health, although in Belgium and Greece the
corresponding ministry is that for social affairs. Responsibility for health is often
combined with other responsibilities. For example, in France there is a Ministry for
Social Affairs, Health and Cities. Spain has a Ministry of Health and Consumer
Affairs and the Netherlands has a Ministry of Welfare, Health and Cultural Affairs.

The boundaries of the competence of the lead ministry vary considerably. The core function is generally seen as the regulation or provision of health services. Differences in the scope and function of ministries largely reflect the different ways of financing and delivering health services and the degree of centralization of responsibility for health services within the Member State. Typically, in countries with national health services, health ministries are involved in the provision of services whereas, in countries with systems based on social insurance, they have a more regulatory role. In Germany, Greece and Portugal, government responsibility for health services is retained centrally in the Ministry of Health whereas in Denmark, responsibility is at the county, with a corresponding diminution in the role of the national ministry. Spain, currently undergoing a process of devolution of health services to the regional level, provides an example of an intermediate position, with health services devolved to six regions, representing 57 per cent of the population, but retention of control at the centre for the remaining parts of the country. A somewhat similar situation pertains in the United Kingdom, with responsibility for health services vested in ministries within each of the constituent countries.

While ministries of health are involved in the regulation or provision of health services for the general population in all Member States, there are a wide variety of bodies providing occupationally-based services for specific groups and under the control of other ministries. The services provided by these bodies vary from the production of guidance on safety at work through monitoring the health of workers through to the provision of curative services. Most Member States have a ministry with responsibility for general issues of health and safety at work. This is normally the Ministry of Labour or Employment. In addition, guidance or monitoring of workplace safety for specific groups may be provided by other ministries. Examples of these groups and the responsible ministries include workers in the nuclear industry (Energy) and farmers (Agriculture). Curative services are typically provided for groups who, by nature of their employment, have reduced access to the general health services. Examples include, in many Member States, the provision of health care for members of the armed forces and prisoners by Defence and Interior Ministries respectively. Other examples result from the specific composition of the workforce in certain Member States. For example, the Greek Ministry of Shipping is responsible for some health services received by merchant sailors and, in Spain, the Instituto Social de la Marina, part of the Ministry of Social Security and Labour Affairs, has certain responsibilities for the health needs of those in the fishing industry. Finally, responsibility for certain categories of the population may reside in a separate ministry for historical reasons, such as the financing of health care for state employees in Spain, which has remained under the control of the Ministry of Public Administration or in Portugal where the civil servants have their own health fund managed by the Ministry of Finance. Some Member States are moving towards greater integration of services. For example, the United Kingdom is examining how to increase links between services provided by the National Health Service and those provided for prisoners and armed forces personnel.

The indistinct dividing line between the health and social needs of the elderly and children has led to variation in the division of responsibilities between ministries where these functions are separated. In Spain, the Ministry of Social Affairs has responsibility for certain aspects of services for the elderly, the handicapped and children. Germany has separate Ministries for Women and Children and for Families and the Elderly.

Member States also differ in the extent to which health ministries have responsibility for regulating the provision of those resources (human, material and intellectual) necessary for health services to function. Undergraduate medical education is undertaken in universities under the authority of Ministries of Education in all Member States, although Ministries of Health have varying levels of involvement in determining student numbers. There is much greater variation in the arrangements for postgraduate medical education. In some Member States this is also the responsibility of the Ministry of Education, through the universities. In Ireland and the United Kingdom autonomous colleges play an important role. Public health medicine has typically attracted a greater level of state involvement than other specialties and this has led to special arrangements for postgraduate training in some Member States that have specialist schools of public health under the authority of Ministries of Health. In some other Member States, public health training is organized in the same way as for other medical specialties, although there is a specific academic component provided by universities.[80] Member States also vary as to whether they have placed training of nurses and other health professionals under the control of the Ministry of Health or Education. Acquisition of the knowledge required to deliver effective health services is typically divided between Ministries of Health and of Research or Science.

Moving beyond health services to the wider determinants of health, responsibilities are similarly dispersed. Road safety is usually the responsibility of Ministries of Transport, although it may come under the aegis of the interior ministry, as in Spain. Environmental protection and food safety are typically the responsibility of a Ministry of the Environment although in Spain they are the responsibility of the Ministry of Infrastructure and Transport and, in England, responsibility for food safety is shared between the Department of Health and the Ministry of Agriculture, Fisheries and Food. Food policy is typically the responsibility of Ministries of Agriculture but is the responsibility of the Ministry of Health in Italy and is shared with the Department of Health in the United Kingdom.

The diversity of government ministries and agencies involved in health has led some Member States to establish formal mechanisms to coordinate activities. In most Member States these have been established to examine specific topics, such as drug abuse, road safety, or AIDS.

A few Member States have created bodies with wider responsibilities for public health. For example, in Denmark, the Ministry of Health has responsibility for coordinating health promotion and disease prevention initiatives, working with an inter-ministerial committee with a core membership but the ability to involve others as required. The Irish Government has a cabinet sub-committee on health promotion involving ministries such as agriculture, industry and environment. In England, an inter-ministerial committee is part of the 'Health of the Nation' initiative and the Chief Medical Officer is the principal medical advisor to all ministries and not just health.

This brief review has highlighted the widely varying natures of Ministries of Health in Member States and the diversity of ministries with responsibility for some of the wider determinants of health. This presents a challenge to those involved in the development of healthy public policies at a European level as different ministries in each Member State may be responsible for a specific policy area.

The role of government

Understanding how policies and priorities developed at European level might be implemented at national level requires a knowledge of the relationship between health services and central government in each Member State. The following paragraphs provide a framework for comparison of the particular circumstances in Member States.

All Member States have decentralized health services to a greater or lesser extent. Four types of decentralization have been described:[81] deconcentration, where functions are managed by local branches of central government; devolution, where functions are devolved to sub-national levels of government that have a degree of independence of central government with respect to certain functions; delegation, where management responsibility for defined functions is delegated to organizations outside the structure of central government and only under its indirect control; and privatization. All of these models are represented, to some extent, among the Member States. The choice of model reflects the views of national governments about the extent to which various aspects of social policy should be planned and/or implemented by government and whether such functions should be the responsibility of local or central government. Each model has different consequences for the ability of governments to introduce new policies and to bring about change.

In both Ireland and the United Kingdom, central government develops priorities for health and health care which are then communicated through a deconcentrated hierarchical system to local health boards or authorities. In England, for example, priorities for the delivery of services are communicated through Regional and District Health Authorities. They are required to develop strategic frameworks for the development of services in the light of these national policies and priorities. In some cases, such as HIV/AIDS and the development of quality assurance, earmarked funds have been provided by central government, although health authorities retain considerable latitude as to how they spend them. In addition to the national priorities developed by the Department of Health, the development of a provider market is increasing the extent to which local priorities are being developed by health authorities. In the wider health context, the achievement of the targets in the 'Health of the Nation' strategy require action by other government ministries and by a wide variety of other bodies although the Department of Health, both centrally and through health authorities, has the lead role in monitoring them. Health authorities often play a leading role in establishing mechanisms to bring together the relevant bodies. The National Health Service Management Executive has issued regions and districts with guidance on how to achieve these targets and the Department of Health has issued handbooks for each key area to assist managers and directors in purchasing authorities to develop local strategies for reducing mortality and morbidity in each area. The handbooks also aim to disseminate information about local initiatives to managers and directors in provider organizations.

In Denmark, which also has a universal health service, responsibility for curative and preventive services is devolved to counties and municipalities. The Ministry does issue guidance and provides advice but it must act through negotiation with the Associations of County Councils and Municipalities. Recent examples include the development of community mental health services and the reduction of hospital waiting lists. The government may make funding available to support these initiatives. Counties and municipalities are responsible for curative as well as preventive services and they are required to prepare plans setting out how they propose to achieve their objectives. For curative services, changes in fee levels are agreed between the Association of County Councils and the Association of General Practitioners. The government has the ability to influence these negotiations through its power to refuse to recognize the agreement. In Italy, the ability of central government to bring about change is also limited by the increased role of the regions, which have considerable autonomy as to how they spend their funding, provided from central government, based on a combination of capitation formulae and historical factors. The situation is more complicated in Spain because of the partial devolution of responsibility for health care. It is not clear that central government has the ability to earmark funds allocated to regions for specific purposes. Both Italy and Spain have set up a planning system to coordinate regional plans into a national plan (see Box 5.1). In Portugal, planning and priority setting are centralized at the Ministry of Health, including the authorization of private facilities. It is expected that the recent creation of five health regions will lead to some decentralization of the planning process.

In Member States with health systems based on sickness funds, the financing and delivery of care is largely delegated or privatized. This reflects, partly, a traditional view of the independence of the liberal professions, including medicine, and partly a response to the almost sacrosanct view of the medical profession in favour of free choice of doctor. However, ministries in all Member States with social insurance systems have retained powers to either promote or block policies agreed by the sickness funds and health care providers. For example, in Belgium, the federal Minister for Social Affairs has negotiated changes in the reimbursement scheme with the 'Institut National d'Assurances contre la Maladie et l'Invalidité', a statutory body containing representatives of health care professionals and 'mutualities', in order to promote changes in the balance of primary and secondary care. In France, similar negotiations take place with the 'Sécurité Sociale'. Further this country approved in 1991 a national plan for capital development (see Box 5.2) and a new process of priority setting is being undertaken by the Ministry of Health using the Delphi Method. In Greece, the Ministry of Health has considerable powers. Although nominally independent, the occupationally-based insurance organizations are very closely linked with government, with their fee schedules governed by legislation that is specific for each organization.

Box 5.1: Planning systems in Italy and Spain

In Italy, a formal national health planning system was established with the introduction of the NHS in 1978. According to the NHS law, a strategic plan would be produced every three years by the government and approved by the parliament. Regional and local plans would then be generated every year based on the guidelines set up in the national plan. However, the lack of parliamentary consensus and other contextual problems delayed this process until 1993, when the first national health plan was officially approved, following a major restructuring of the Italian political system and reform of the NHS. This plan sets up priority areas for action and determines basic standards of health care which must be guaranteed in all Italian regions. The allocation of financial resources to regions is based on per capita criteria with which regions will meet the standards set at national level. The regions can provide services above these standards, but any additional expenditure incurred would have to be met out of their own resources.

Similarly, Spain introduced a National Health Planning System with the creation of the National Health Service in 1986. A major concern underlying the planning system was the need to set common objectives and coordinate the highly decentralized regional health services. By 1993, the devolution of health services had taken place in six out of the 17 regions. Following a traditional planning cycle, the Ministry of Health would produce national guidelines which would be taken into account by regions and health areas for the production of health plans. The national plan would then be the result of aggregating regional plans. In 1989, the Ministry of Health produced national guidelines for the elaboration of health plans termed General Criteria for Health Coordination. Since then several regions have approved regional plans, yet a complete planning cycle, involving all organizational tiers, and regions has not yet taken place. The Ministry of Health in August 1993 produced the fifth draft of the National Health Plan for consultation.

Box 5.2: Planning in France

Before 1991, the only way to regulate capital developments in France was through the 'health map' which laid down quantitative limits for expensive medical technologies and for hospitals beds for each geographical area. Since 1991, a new system of qualitative planning has been added at regional level. All health institutions will have to produce their own plans and these will be developed by committees into a regional plan (SROS). Some specific activities, however, will continue to be planned at the central level – such as neurosurgery, transplants and certain cardiac surgery.

In 1983 the Dutch State Secretary for Welfare, Health and Cultural Affairs established a Steering Committee for Future Health Scenarios. This committee set up a series of commissions to which individuals were appointed in a personal, rather than a representative capacity. Topics were selected on the basis of social relevance and the scope for future research and related to diseases, determinants of health, or methods of health care delivery. The resulting reports provided a basis for decision-making by politicians, insurance organizations, and health care professionals. On 1 January 1994 this committee was privatized.

Devolution and delegation operate in Germany, where priorities for curative care arise largely as a result of negotiations between sickness funds and the medical profession at Land or sub-Land level. Some sickness funds, such as those in France and Germany, have developed health promotion activities. In other Member States, these activities may be organized separately by local government, as in Belgium. In both cases, priorities developed by central government must be negotiated. In France, the situation is somewhat less clear as responsibilities for preventive health and health promotion have been, relatively recently, delegated to local government, the 'Conseils généraux', but the exact division of responsibilities is still under discussion.

The constraints on central government and the decentralized nature of health promotion and health services in most Member States have provided a fertile basis for the development of a large number of local initiatives. A few, such as the WHO Healthy Cities and Healthy Regions projects, have spread throughout Member States. These have stimulated the development of comprehensive local health plans. Box 5.3 shows examples from Germany, Denmark, Spain and Greece. Others have been confined to one area or have spread throughout the country of origin. Member States vary in the extent to which these initiatives have arisen and the amount and nature of support provided for them. In some Member States, governments have established mechanisms to encourage such initiatives (see Box 5.4, for examples).

The United Kingdom Department of Health, seeks to encourage the evaluation of local initiatives and dissemination of information on them through its research

Box 5.3: Healthy Cities and Healthy Regions

The health services in the city of Copenhagen have published a comprehensive review of the health needs of their population,[82] setting out principles for health promotion, the importance of social networks for health, the diversity of health promotion settings, and developing themes for health promotion in Copenhagen. The resulting plans involve all relevant sectors and are the responsibility of an inter-departmental steering group within the City Council.

In Spain, the Healthy Cities initiative began in 1986 and there are now 22 cities integrated in this network. There are also plans to set up the Iberoamerican network of healthy cities integrating Spain, Portugal and Latin American countries. In 1988, a national office was set up for the coordination of this initiative, diffusion of information and common areas for action were established. Two national conferences were held in 1989 and 1990. In 1991, five common working areas were defined: health inequalities, development of individual skills, building a healthy environment, reorientation of health services and health policy for healthy cities.

In France, the programme started in 1988 and now covers 34 cities. France also participates in a French-speaking Healthy Cities network.

In Greece, the city of Patras has established a centre to:
• mobilize the citizens and ensure their participation in solving their public health problems;
• develop mechanisms for inter-sectoral approaches to health policies;
• prepare a health plan for the city;
• collaborate with other cities in the programme on individual public health and health promotion projects.

In Germany, an initiative on healthy cities was established in Dusseldorf in November 1992. The regions participating in the WHO Healthy Regions Programme from Member States are the Flemmish community in Belgium, Catalonia and Valencia from Spain, Nord Rhine-Westphalia and Lower Saxony from Germany, Grand-Sud-Ouest from France and Wales. The aims are to work together to bring about health gains, to transfer knowledge on the promotion of excellence and effectiveness, the elimination of waste and unnecessary duplication and involve everyone in inter-sectoral action. Nord Rhine-Westphalia is participating not only in the Healthy Regions programme of WHO but also in the ENS CARE project of the EU. It has recently compiled a detailed statistical review in which data are related to the Health for All targets.[83]

and development strategy. In addition, substantial earmarked funds have been used to support local initiatives in specific topics such as HIV/AIDS care, prevention and quality assurance.

In Italy, the Lombardy region has recently funded a major research programme on the future of health care services in the city of Milan. This programme has been undertaken by the School of Medicine of the University of Milan and the Centre for Health Care Management and Economics of Bocconi University. The underlying assumption is that the provision of health care in large cities encounters distinctive health and organizational problems with health services run by different local authorities and several self-governing hospitals. Different organizational frameworks and their likely impact on the health of the population are being studied. Proposals for establishing a public hospital network similar to those operating in Paris and New York are being considered.

Box 5.4: Encouraging local initiatives in Denmark

In the last decade innovative local initiatives have been seen as an important tool in bringing about changes in health care. Introducing an innovation as a local initiative is often more acceptable than doing so nationally. The Danish Ministry of Health provides support, through a Health Project Fund, for the dissemination of information and funding to initiate and evaluate local initiatives. As a result, many features of the Danish health care system began locally but subsequently spread throughout the health system. These include the development of 24 hour home nursing care, preventive visits by home nurses to elderly people, health promotion in general practice, and community mental health centres. Each year, priority areas are identified by the Ministry of Health. An important element is the willingness of local bodies to provide co-financing and the likely long-term viability of the project after the cessation of state assistance.

These few examples show the complexity of setting and implementing priorities in pluralistic societies and highlight the important role of local initiatives. Although circumstances vary between Member States, many of these local initiatives tackle common problems and much can be learnt from them. Other than in a few specific areas, such as HIV/AIDS, it is often difficult to obtain information on them outside the Member State involved.

Involving the public

There are three principal means of involving the public in the development of health policies: through the representative democratic process; through organized interest groups; and through direct involvement of individual citizens.

In all Member States, the public's views are expressed through the representative democratic process. Primary legislation undergoes scrutiny during its passage through parliament. In addition, all Member States have some form of standing parliamentary committee that examines health-related legislation and its implementation. Other mechanisms involving the democratic process include management of health services by local government, as in Denmark and the creation of statutory advisory committees such as the Area Health Councils in Spain, consisting of representatives of trade unions and local government, and the Community Health Councils in the United Kingdom, whose members are nominated by local government (half), voluntary organizations (one third) and regional health authorities (one sixth).

The extent to which consumer organizations have developed varies widely among Member States, largely as a result of historical factors. In general, their roles are greatest in Ireland, the Netherlands, and the United Kingdom and least in the Southern European countries. In the Netherlands, the involvement of consumer groups is relatively formalized, with participation by the Dutch Federation of Patients and Consumers in many decision-making processes. In the United Kingdom, consumer organizations are consulted at all stages in the development and implementation of policy by central government through to district health authorities. Throughout the Union, the role of consumer organizations is increasing, often with support from the mass media, and there is a growing tendency to challenge the ways in which care is provided. An example was a publication by a French magazine that questioned the adequacy of emergency care in certain hospitals. The particular factors associated with HIV/AIDS, such as its impact on a relatively young and vocal population and the reaction to episodes of contaminated blood and blood products, have led to the growth of new consumer movements, often with specific national characteristics.

The views of consumers may also be represented through trade unions. Their role also varies considerably, typically being greater in those countries, such as Germany, France and Luxembourg where they are involved in the management of sickness funds. In other Member States they are often involved in formal advisory bodies. Trade unions often have an important role in promoting health and safety at work. In some Member States, such as the United Kingdom, where they are no longer included in the membership of health authorities, their role has been reduced considerably.

There have been relatively few attempts to involve the public directly in developing health policies, although at least two Member States have developed mechanisms to do so. In the United Kingdom, the statement that health authorities are responsible for meeting the health needs of their populations has stimulated some to undertake public consultation, some of them drawing on the experience of the Oregon experiment (see Box 5.5), to determine the views of their local population, although these attempts have been criticized by others who have drawn attention to the limited representativeness of those taking part. The committee which prepared the health policy strategy for France held debates in four large cities attended by 246 to 300 people, including the medical profession, administrators, social security organizations, elected representatives, trade unions and consumer organizations.

The discussion of the Dunning Report[84] in the Netherlands, summarized below, has also involved a process of public consultation. A central Communication Office is coordinating a public education campaign which, according to the mandate of the Dunning Committee, aims to 'get a discussion going, through third parties, on the question of whether all that is possible in health care should in fact be done. The aim of this discussion is to introduce the public to the idea of the need for making choices'. The 'communication plan' makes explicit the main routes of communication with the public, as well as the approach which is more communicative than informative.

The process involved a series of projects, one of which, entitled 'Health Care Choices from the Patient's Perspective', was organized by the Dutch Federation of Patients and Consumers Association. This project consisted of two main parts. In the first, a series of meetings was held in which a video on health choices was shown and questions were asked about the way in which patients interact with the health care system and how they make their own choices. The responses were analysed and used to generate a choice map that indicated how important each choice was to them. Preliminary results suggest that patients do not necessarily want more health care but rather to have greater autonomy in making choices. In the second, a series of checklists were designed for use by patients when consulting a doctor to assist them to obtain the maximum amount of information about what the doctor proposes.

Trying to involve the public raises a number of difficulties. In the United Kingdom, one community survey carried out by City and Hackney Health Authority asked the public to rank either broad groups of services or specific treatments[85] (see Box 5.5). Examples of the former included long stay care for the elderly, preventive services such as screening and immunization, and medical research into new treatments. Examples of more specific services included treatments for infertility, family planning services, and cosmetic surgery. The surveyors compared the priorities indicated by the public, with those decided by hospital doctors, primary care doctors and public health doctors. They found that the rankings given by the public were quite different in some cases from those given by health professionals. This finding has been a feature of similar work.

Crucially, the surveyors in City and Hackney found that the wording and information given in the questions asked affected the ranking given by the public. For example 'intensive care for premature babies' was ranked higher than 'intensive care for babies weighing less than one and a half pounds and unlikely to survive'. Therefore both prior knowledge and information given by surveyors is likely to have an important effect on public preferences elicited in such exercises. Asking the public questions about broad service groups may be more meaningful than asking them to rank specific treatments.

But as it is difficult to elicit meaningful preferences from public consultation exercises and to incorporate these into decisions about priorities, public consultation may be used to give legitimacy to controversial priorities made by priority setters, and vice versa. Public education campaigns could also be used to make political decisions more palatable. Nor is it clear that the public at large want to be involved in decisions about priorities. For example a recent MORI survey in the United Kingdom[86] showed that, of the 2012 people surveyed, most preferred to leave the decision-making to health professionals, health service managers and to a lesser extent politicians rather than to the public. On the other hand, a recent survey of Health Authorities in the United Kingdom reported that priority setters did not use the public's judgement about priorities even if they had access to it.[87] Paradoxically, the survey also showed that health authorities felt that this information was useful to help set priorities.

Box 5.5: Examples of attempts at public involvement in the United Kingdom

a) North Essex Health Consortium

354 people were interviewed face to face in their homes. This exercise revealed biases towards treating larger numbers of people at the expense of people with severe conditions, towards children rather than the elderly. Critical life-saving care was accorded top priority unless the patient was elderly, prevention and treatment of mental illness and care for chronic conditions were both rated highly, whereas short term elective treatment was a low priority. The health authority concluded that the public were prepared to prioritize health care, although there was a reluctance to make explicit choices.[88]

b) Kensington Chelsea and Westminster Health Authority

In a health and lifestyle survey of 500 residents of this health authority, respondents were interviewed face to face on a range of questions related to their health status and behaviours, and use of health services. In addition, interviewees were asked to rank a list of 25 health care treatments and services by selecting the five most important for funding and the five least important. While the majority of respondents identified their five most important services, only 32 could identify the five least important. The most favoured priorities for funding were education to prevent the spread of AIDS and high-technology surgery such as transplants. The three services chosen by the fewest respondents as priorities for funding were abortion, fertility treatment, and hernia repair.

c) City and Hackney Health Authority

City and Hackney Health Authority undertook a survey using face to face questionnaires. Respondents were asked to list 16 health services on a priority ranging from essential to less important. Most people valued high-technology surgery and life-saving treatments as the number one priority. For instance, heart transplants, treatments for people with leukaemia, and preventive services such as immunizations, blood pressure screening and so on came high on people's priority list. At the bottom of the list were cosmetic surgery, infertility treatments, health education and family planning.

Provider groups

Several provider groups have an important role in shaping health policy although their role and importance vary among Member States. These are the health care professions, especially the medical profession, the pharmaceutical and medical technology industries, and the sickness funds. Their involvement may be within the context of specific initiatives, in the organization and delivery of health services, such as the Greek Central Council of Health or the Dutch National Council for Public Health, or in more wide-ranging assessment of social policy, sometimes also involving consumer groups, such as the Irish Programme for Economic and Social Progress.

In most Member States, the medical profession continues to play an important part in this process although, in many cases, this is declining as part of a more general challenge to professional autonomy. Its influence varies considerably, as do the issues on which it has sought to exert pressure. This is partly because of the diversity in perceived function by different medical organizations, some of which act as trade unions, such as the British Medical Association or the French 'Ordre des Médecins'. In Germany there are several organizations of professionals with differing, though overlapping functions. The 'Kassenärztliche Vereinigungen', has a principal concern for their members' financial and employment interests. The Irish and British Colleges are more concerned with quality of care and have been particularly active in developing guidelines and producing reports on areas of apparent unmet need or inadequate provision of prevention or care. In Germany, the Bundesausschuß plays a similar role (see Box 5.6). The divisions are not rigid and some of the former, such as the British Medical Association, have campaigned vigorously against certain threats to health such as tobacco.

Box 5.6: The Bundesausschuß in Germany

This consists of 9 representatives of the doctors and 9 of the insurance funds plus 2 independent members. Its task is to make sure that the public receives sufficient, adequate and efficient treatment, with special emphasis on the mentally ill. Guidelines are published on, for example:

- treatments by doctors;
- measures for early recognition of disease;
- medical care for pregnancy and childbirth;
- new diagnostic and treatment methods;
- prescriptions of drugs, hospital care and home care;
- judgements on incapacity for work;
- facility planning;
- medical measures to induce pregnancy.

The pharmaceutical and medical equipment industries are, arguably, among the most important influences on the organization and delivery of health care. In many Member States, the absence of an explicitly defined research strategy and limited government funding for research means that industry is the major force in directing research. As a consequence, research effort is directed towards those treatments and investigations that have commercial potential rather than those that are actually needed to improve the health of the population. This has led to, for example, high levels of investment in the development of drugs with negligible advantages over those already in use and under-investment in research on preparations which either have no patent protection as they are already in use, even though they may have new and important applications, or in drugs which are needed only by those without the resources to pay for them, such as many drugs for tropical diseases. There is also some concern about the extent to which commercially-sponsored research may be associated with selective, and thus misleading publications.[89] There has been considerable opposition to some attempts to develop systematic overviews of evidence, especially where they indicate that new preparations have little or no advantage over existing ones.

Industry also directs priorities through promotional budgets. While these are often used legitimately there has also been recent concern in some countries that some payments may have been made illegally.[90] More recently, the pharmaceutical industry in some countries has adopted a broader approach, seeking to influence political decisions on the structure of health care systems in ways that will benefit it.[91]

Sickness funds may have an important influence on priorities through their decisions on levels of reimbursement and coverage of services. District health authorities in the United Kingdom, through their purchasing function, are likely to develop in a similar way. The degree of government control over the level of coverage and rates of reimbursement offered by sickness funds varies. In general, sickness funds have concentrated their attention on curative services but they are increasingly developing preventive activities. Examples include the introduction, on an evaluative basis, of screening for breast and colon cancer in some French 'départements'. Similarly the Luxembourg sickness funds pay for breast cancer screening. The Ministry of Health coordinates this programme and pays the administrative costs. In Germany, most screening programmes are paid for by the sickness funds. The important role played by purchasers and providers of health care makes it essential to involve them in the development of health-related policies. In many Member States their involvement has been largely in the field of curative services.

Research-based evidence

The provision of preventive and curative services in Member States is based heavily on research-based evidence, commonly through incorporating published research in the development of treatments and programmes. In addition, however, some

Member States have taken a more proactive approach by either undertaking epidemiological overviews of the health of their populations which can inform the development of health services and policies or by developing research strategies which identify gaps in current knowledge, seek to fill them, and disseminate the results.

The extent to which epidemiological information is used to shape priorities and policies appears to vary considerably. One manifestation of this is the publication of systematic reports on the population's health. Such a report has been published by the chief medical officers of the constituent countries of the United Kingdom for over a century and districts and regions are now also required to produce annual reports that are public and should be used to inform purchasing strategies and health promotion activities. Many examples are now available from other Member States, often as part of Health for All strategies. Programmes such as the WHO Healthy Cities and Healthy Regions have been particularly influential in this process. These reports provide an important source of information for those involved in developing priorities, by highlighting the major challenges to health in a specific area.

All Member States have mechanisms for funding health-related research. Typically there are multiple sources of funding, including government ministries, research councils, and industry. This diversification has many advantages, but it also makes it difficult to develop mechanisms that ensure that the results of research meet the health needs of the population and are used to improve the provision of care. While ministries of health in all Member States commission research to solve specific problems, there are few examples of systematic reviews of national strategy in health-related research and development.

Selected examples of such strategies include an international review of research activity undertaken by the Danish National Research Council which has produced proposals for strengthening research in health services, epidemiology, biochemistry, and cardiovascular disease. An international evaluation of Danish health services research and epidemiology took place in 1992. A data base was established at the Danish Institute of Clinical Epidemiology which published a catalogue in English of 391 projects conducted between 1989 and 1991. The most common topics were the evaluation of treatment and prevention covering 30 per cent of projects followed by health economics with 9 per cent of projects.[92]

In addition, the Danish National Board of Health in collaboration with scientific societies, has a programme of developing practice guidelines based on systematic reviews of research-based evidence. In Germany, the Ministry of Health launched in April 1993 'Health research 2000' with emphasis on environment, nutrition, life styles and the health problems of the elderly, women and other populations at risk. In Greece, the Ministry of Health is planning to establish a National Centre for Health Research in 1995; it will have departments on medical informatics, health planning, biomedical technology, evaluation, epidemiology, health promotion and communicable diseases. The United Kingdom Department of Health launched a national research and development strategy in 1991. This seeks to ensure that the content and delivery of care in the National Health Service is based on high quality research relevant to improving the health of the nation. A Central Research and Development Committee advises on priorities based on input from managers and health care professionals, coordinated through regions. As part of this process, there is a series of systematic reviews of research priorities in areas such as mental health and cardiovascular disease and stroke. Working within these national guidelines, regional committees will identify and develop their own programmes with a focus on areas of local interest, ensuring co-ordination with other regions and with other bodies funding health-related research to avoid duplication. A task force was set up in November 1993 to review the ways in which the NHS currently funds research and development.

A recent report on health research in the Netherlands[93] proposes that medical research should be reorganized along the lines of that in the United Kingdom with five streams of funding as shown in Box 5.7.

Box 5.7: Streams of funding health research proposed for the Netherlands

1. Basic funding should be used for the physical infrastructure or for various institutions to build up their knowledge base.
2. Funds for universities and institutes for innovative science-driven research.
3. Funds for gaps in research identified by the Ministry of Education and Sciences.
4. Funds from the Ministry of Public Health to build up the knowledge base for problem-oriented research.
5. Funds for developing, monitoring, evaluating and disseminating a system of problem-focused research.

Several of these initiatives seek to tackle the problem of making maximum use of existing research. Many studies are too small to provide conclusive results on their own but, when combined, have sufficient statistical power to provide a much more reliable answer. A major international collaborative programme has recently been established to co-ordinate the activities of centres undertaking these reviews. The Cochrane Collaboration includes several centres in the Union as well as others in North America and Australia.

6

Systematic Approaches to Establishing Priorities

Introduction

At present services are often allocated on a first come, first served basis. Those who do not come do not receive services. There is considerable underuse of effective health interventions and considerable failure to comply with treatments which are provided, for example, drugs not taken as directed. It would clearly be unacceptable to allocate scarce service by giving patients random numbers. But the use of very advanced procedures could be restricted to those who could benefit most from them. Such criteria could be medical or social. Social criteria might be age, occupation, family status or economic status. Only the first deserves some consideration. Should the wish of the patient and the family to withhold life-prolonging treatment from an elderly person in pain with only the prospect of a few more weeks of life be respected? In some countries there is already denial of some treatments to elderly persons on the grounds that they are unlikely to survive the intervention or have diminished capacity to withstand post-operative complications. Are such decisions best left informal? Should treatment be denied when a psychiatric illness or behaviour pattern is likely to interfere significantly with compliance?

There are many potential ways of limiting the services provided. Should governments avoid financing research into the development of new technologies? Should there be stringent assessments of new technologies before they are allowed to be disseminated? Should all Member States have effective means of preventing the dissemination of technologies in response to market forces not only in hospitals but outside? This follows the lines of the health maps applied in Belgium and France. The purposes would be to restrict use to centres with the skill to use them appropriately, to remove temptations to use them for purposes for which there is no gain in outcome, and to reduce to the minimum the under-utilization of expensive equipment. The restriction would also apply to gifts of equipment and leasing arrangements.

Should the services which are publicly financed be restricted to 'core' services, leaving other services wholly for private payment? There already have been moves in this direction as mentioned earlier. They include the removal of spa treatment from the fee schedule, cutting out cosmetic surgery, not financing dental bridges or spectacles for adults unless they have very bad sight, not reimbursing a range of over-the-counter drugs, and heavy increases in cost-sharing for dentistry or 'comfort' drugs and reductions in subsidies to travel costs.

If the restriction to core services is to go deeper, there needs to be explicit criteria to define the 'core'. The question arises of whether consideration should be given to the possibility of excluding some services or only new treatments, high cost treatments or high volume low cost treatments. The implicit criteria behind the actions so far taken are that the costs are low, that the condition cannot be life-threatening, that the medical value is not clearly established or the provision can be readily abused and that, as there is no urgency, patients can be expected to save up to pay the cost e.g. for adult dentistry. These criteria are used unevenly between Member States. The criterion of low cost raises the possibility of targeting on those for whom the cost, though low for the average family, could be a burden for those with very low incomes or not so low incomes and large families. The difficulty with this is that, while a distinction can be made for those receiving social assistance, not all those eligible claim and it would be administratively difficult to find those in an income range just above this level.

This chapter describes three main methodological approaches to priority setting, examines how Member States establish priorities in practice, and finally reviews five systematic approaches to priority setting which attempt to define a package of core services.

Some methodological approaches to priority setting

The need to set priorities against a background of health needs and limited resources has stimulated interest in epidemiological and economic methodological approaches. Some of these appear, at first sight, to offer a means of comparing different programmes and interventions. They are, however, subject to certain methodological constraints and involve controversial value judgements. A particular concern is the ways in which inputs and outputs should be valued. The following paragraphs provide a brief summary of some of the issues surrounding three such approaches – burden of disease, cost benefit and cost utility analysis.

Burden of disease
This approach is based on the view that those problems which present the greatest challenge to health should be given the highest priority. This is often used when a professional group is advancing the case for priority being given to 'their' disease. Unfortunately, there are many ways of measuring the burden of disease, each producing different answers. As a result, the approach is of very limited value in set-

ting priorities, although it is discussed here because it is widely used in practice. The criteria adopted may be the impact of the disease in terms of mortality, morbidity, financial cost, the availability of effective treatment, or its potential for increase in the absence of prevention or treatment. These will be considered in turn.

There are many ways of measuring the impact of a disease on mortality. Total numbers of deaths from a condition pay insufficient attention to the fact that everyone must die from something eventually. They also have the effect of emphasizing the contribution of degenerative diseases. As a consequence, the concept of premature death has been proposed, in which either the number of years of life lost or the number of deaths before a certain age is calculated. The variation in the natural history of different diseases means that the identification of the 'most important' cause of death is highly sensitive to the age cut-off chosen. For example, the use of the age 50 will emphasize the importance of accidents, whereas the age 65 will emphasize heart disease and 75 will emphasize cancer. In practice, the three or four leading causes of death are the same with all approaches, although their ordering may differ.

As an illustration, the number of premature deaths that would be saved if death rates from specific causes among those under 65 could be reduced throughout the Union to the levels seen in those countries where they are lowest has been calculated (Table 6.1).

A method that combines this concept with priority setting based on the availability of effective interventions is that of avoidable deaths. These are a basic measure of health care performance and consist of certain conditions from which people should not die before a certain age (usually 65) if they are given appropriate treatment at the right time. Such deaths may reflect a failure to provide quality curative and preventive medical care.

The European Community's working group on avoidable deaths produced a series of atlases of avoidable deaths.[94] For the first atlas, seventeen conditions were selected by international consensus. Three of them reflected national health policy e.g. on cigarette smoking to prevent lung cancer. The remaining fourteen disease groups reflected both primary and secondary care. Mortality was considered within strict age-limits so as to enhance the validity of mortality as a measure of health service outcome. In Table 6.2, the findings for five conditions in the period 1980-84 are given for illustration to show the extent of variation between Member States. The conditions not shown in the Table are: malignant neoplasm of the cervix uteri, Hodgkin's disease, chronic rheumatic heart disease, abdominal hernia, cholelithiasis and cholecystitis, hypertensive and cerebrovascular diseases, maternal mortality, and perinatal mortality.

Even more striking was the variation within Member States although accurate comparisons of measures of dispersion of the ranges cannot be made because of the differences in the size of the population in the administrative areas used as the basis of data collection.

Partly due to changes in classification, the study recorded a fall of avoidable mortality between 1974-78 and 1980-84 for all conditions studied, except asthma for which there was a 27 per cent increase. When the data were analysed by age groups, there was still a fall except in the case of cancer of the cervix for which there were both increases and decreases in different age groups.

Table 6.1: Deaths avoided annually if all regions attained the optimal level*

Volume 1 (1980-84)

Disease	Age range	Country with lowest rate	Deaths saved annually
Tuberculosis	5-64	Luxembourg	2497
Malignant neoplasm of cervix uteri	15-64	Italy	2426
Malignant neoplasm of cervic and body of uterus	15-64	Netherlands	1209
Hodgkin's disease	5-64	Luxembourg	657
Chronic rheumatic heart disease	5-44	Belgium	761
All respiratory diseases	1-14	France	668
Asthma	5-44	Spain	742
Appendicitis	5-64	Greece	219
Abdominal hernia	5-64	Greece	294
Cholelithiasis and cholecystitis	5-64	Scotland	834
Hypertensive and cerebrovascular diseases	35-64	Netherlands	16409
Maternal deaths	all	Luxembourg	474
Perinatal mortality	<1 week + still	Denmark	16662
Total avoidable deaths saved annually			**43852**

* Potential effect of reducing the death rates in all Member States to that of the lowest. Data are from most recent available year (varies among countries but all are 1989, 1990, or 1991) derived from WHO HFA data-base.

Source: W. Holland, *European Community Atlas of Avoidable Deaths*, (second edition), Oxford, 1991.

The incidence of avoidable deaths tends to decline over time. This appears to be partly due to an improvement in socioeconomic conditions and partly due to an improvement in the quality of health care: at least the incidence of deaths from avoidable conditions declines faster than for other conditions.

Table 6.2: Standard mortality ratios based on an EU Standard (1980-84)

Country	Condition				
	Asthma	Acute resp. disease ages 1-4	Appendicitis	Uterus cancers*	Tuber-culosis
Belgium	170	78	49	80	61
Germany	185	78	128	97	84
Denmark	75	59	104	159	36
Spain	41	117	108	88	181
France	68	53	112	92	97
Greece	–	104	41	84	121
Italy	27	112	96	100	103
Ireland	180	115	94	73	160
Luxembourg	134	57	188	99	26
Netherlands	62	57	83	68	27
Portugal	–	275	136	129	313
UK: E&W	170	123	69	124	53
UK: NI	187	135	94	112	52
UK: Scotland	148	108	79	126	81
EU	100	100	100	100	100

* Malignant neoplasm of cervix and body of uterus.

Source: W. Holland, *European Community Atlas of Avoidable Deaths*, (second edition), Oxford, 1991.

The second volume of the atlas included eight further conditions for which death was considered partly avoidable given timely and appropriate care. The second volume considered: intestinal infections, cancer of the breast, cancer of the skin, cancer of the testis, leukaemias, ischaemic heart disease, peptic ulcers, and congenital cardiovascular anomalies. Once again there was considerable variation both between and within Member States. In Portugal, over 1000 people aged under 15 died of intestinal infections – ten times the overall European Union rate. Five countries had mortality rates for rheumatic heart disease less than half the European Union average and three countries had a mortality rate more than twice the EU average.

The variations found in these studies show numbers of deaths from many conditions which are unacceptably high. For example, over the period 1980-84, deaths from tuberculosis in England and Wales in the age range 5-64 amounted to 1417. Even so, this was half the number expected, judged by average age-specific rates throughout the whole Community. There was no apparent correlation with the quantities of health services provided, such as the density of doctors or acute hospital beds. This may be because further health resources lead to more discretionary procedures and not an increase in procedures for life-threatening conditions which are performed anyway. It is suggested that, once a certain basic standard of services is achieved, it is the accessibility of services which determines, at least in part, the level of avoidable deaths. This would fit with the variation by social class if the lower social classes find it more difficult or are less likely to make use of the services provided.

The collection of data on avoidable deaths identifies problem areas and thus priorities for action to explain the excess mortality and try to prevent it. For example, it was found from the examination of case records that, in one health district in the United Kingdom, women who had died of cancer of the cervix had not undergone screening, despite an adequate call-recall procedure. Variations in admission rates for asthma were examined in 20 areas and it was found that part of the explanation was the availability of services and part was due to higher needs. It was found that among three districts the one with the highest stroke mortality also had the highest incidence of stroke, partly due to the higher proportion of persons of Afro-Caribbean origin who are known to be particularly liable to develop stroke. This suggests a need for greater preventive action and improved rehabilitation services.

All studies of mortality are subject to certain reservations, although the work on avoidable mortality has made strenuous efforts to overcome them. Some of the variation is due to national differences in diagnostic labelling.[95] This is especially true of deaths from suicide but also ischaemic heart disease, chronic bronchitis and liver disease. A reduction in some causes of death, especially those predominantly affecting young people, will lead to a greater population at risk from other diseases. Moreover, the contribution of genetic factors may limit the extent to which a change may be possible and there is increasing evidence that many diseases, such as ischaemic heart disease and hypertension, are influenced by factors acting either in utero or early childhood.[96] Consequently, the impact of any change in public health policy may have a long time lag.

Diseases may also be considered important because of their effect on morbidity. This is normally assessed in terms of measures such as days or years with reduced health status. The third measure, health status, has been combined with mortality data to create the Disability Adjusted Life Year (DALY). This has been used by the World Bank in the 1993 World Development Report to assess the impact of a wide variety of diseases throughout the world.[97] Measures based on morbidity give a greater prominence to chronic diseases and mental health. This concept is considered further under cost-utility analysis.

The importance of a disease may also be considered in terms of the associated financial cost, both direct, in terms of costs to health services, and indirect, in terms of costs to society. This approach is subject to many problems of measurement.

Finally, diseases may be seen as a priority because, even though they do not cause a substantial amount or mortality or morbidity at present, they may do so if appropriate action is not taken. Examples include infectious diseases against which immunization is available, and prevention of HIV infection and AIDS.

The new approaches

All of these approaches have limitations. One of the most important is that they do not seek, explicitly, to reconcile costs and benefits. Two approaches that do so, cost-benefit and cost-utility analysis, will now be considered.

Cost-benefit analysis

In other fields cost-benefit analysis has been used to compare the monetary costs with the monetary gains. If the gains are greater than the costs, the activity is worth financing. Where this has been applied to health services, the costs have been compared with monetary gains calculated in terms of earnings foregone with the earnings in future years discounted to current values. Costs can include the costs of treatment, travel costs and costs to the patient in the time used to receive treatment. The rationale for discounting is that people place a higher value on benefits this year than in the future. Sometimes an allowance has been made for the value of the unpaid 'work' of caring for dependent persons (e.g. children) and for housework. How to value the latter is controversial and it is hard to cost time for someone who is not in paid work, for example the unemployed, the elderly and children. Putting a monetary value on the real or potential gains of treatment is equally controversial and requires value judgements which may not be acceptable to the public at large. Similarly, there is no 'right' answer on the interest rate to choose for discounting future earnings to current values and such calculations are very sensitive to such choices.

Calculations can be made in terms of costs to the patient or the government or society as a whole. The latter would include expenditure on social welfare and social security payments and reductions in income tax as well as the cost of publicly financed health care. This method expressly assumes that the value of each individual's life consists simply in the earnings that individual is commanding. The losses to society may be different from lost earnings if work can be postponed or a worker readily replaced from those unemployed. The retired and those with no jobs and no prospect of obtaining work because of disability or lack of skill have no value at all. Treatments which leave the disabled still too disabled to work are not worth financing. The results are inevitably biased towards the healthy and the more skilled young. Calculations of this kind were made in the early days of attempts to use cost-benefit analysis. While this type of calculation is of value in appraising a commercial investment, the underlying value judgements would not be accepted by public opinion, when applied to health care. Thus some other means needs to be found of calculating benefits.

Cost-utility analysis
Cost-utility analysis seeks to value the benefits of health services in terms of healthy years of life gained rather than in financial terms. Years of less than full health can be counted as proportions of a healthy life year. Thus it is assumed that years of healthy life are of the same value in different individuals. Some may argue that certain periods of life are more valuable than others, for example, early parenthood or when caring for elderly relatives and some may feel it a greater loss to forego the period when their earnings peak. If any of these arguments were accepted, weights could be used before the final stage of comparing the costs of treatments with the value of years gained and shown as a ratio. It is possible for estimates to be made of the average states people will be in after the treatment and how long on average they can be expected to live. It should, however, be remembered that these are estimates and that they are averages: some may have the prospect of responding to the treatment much better than others, the young may progress much better than the aged and so on. The frail, aged and disabled may start with a lower quality of life and thus have less to gain from an intervention.

One such scale used to some extent and much discussed in the United Kingdom is the Rosser scale.[98] Values are put on health states of physical disability ranging from 1 (no disability) to 0 (dead) and from A (no distress) to D (severe distress). Looking only at disability and distress gives a narrow view of health: it ignores such considerations as marriage satisfaction, sexual functioning and reproductive ability unless they cause distress. It is a negative measure rather than the more positive measure of 'feeling well'. It ignores the burden which can fall on other family members.[99] Criticisms can be levelled against any scale on the grounds of incompleteness, but it would take many years of very costly research if the attempt were made to use more comprehensive attempts to measure the quality of life such as the Nottingham Health Profile or the Sickness Impact Profile and to use clinical trials to determine the efficacy of each treatment in terms of healthy life years gained.

But the main problem is who should decide how states of disability (such as not being able to do heavy housework or being in a wheel chair) and other indications of ill-health should be rated? Who should determine degrees of pain and distress? How should disability and distress be weighted? Should the rating be done by a random population sample, by those actually having the degree of disability or pain, by health professionals or by those responsible for determining the priorities? Each would give different results. Doctors were found in a small study to place emphasis on distress, while patients felt disability more important.[100] Again it should be remembered that people vary in how they react to handicaps. For example, some live a full life from a wheel chair, while others restrict their lives.

These indices usually predict the likely improvement in the state of health after a treatment, the value placed on that improvement, and the likely duration of that improvement. The first major criticism is that, because duration of improvement is taken into account, setting priorities within or between treatments would bias against the elderly. Secondly, many other factors are not taken into account in quality of life measures, for example co-morbidities or other factors which may influence a patient's ability to improve. Thirdly, the predicted improvement of a treatment is estimated as the average likely improvement. Certain individuals may be more likely to benefit from treatment far more than others. This potential to benefit more may be predictable in advance but is not included in quality of life measures. Fourthly, the effectiveness of treatments are not fully known and tools to measure improvement still need to be refined and used systematically. The same is true of quality of life measures especially when these tools are being used to help set priorities between a range of different services. Not all research into quality of life for specific treatments is done according to strict definitions, making comparisons of results difficult.

This section reviews seven examples of approaches to priority setting – attempts to define a package of services to be collectively financed. The first example comes from the United States and attempts to apply cost-utility analysis – the Oregon Medicaid reform. The others are the basic package of care defined in the US national health insurance plan, reports of committees on priorities in Norway and Sweden, the report of the New Zealand committee set up to define core services, proposals to establish priorities in Spain and Germany and the report of the Dunning committee in the Netherlands.

The Oregon Medicaid reform

Medicaid, the scheme in the United States for providing health insurance for the poor only covers certain defined categories of poor persons. Because of the cost of the scheme, states have been cutting eligibility levels and reducing the rates paid to doctors. The Oregon reform started as part of a wider initiative to extend health insurance to nearly the whole population of the state, including all below the poverty line. It was decided that it would not be affordable to offer all possible health care to all the poor. Thus it was decided that health care interventions needed to be ranked in order of priority so that the state could finance the more important items to the extent determined by the available funds. To establish this list a Health Service Commission was set up, consisting of five doctors, one public health nurse, one social worker and four representatives of consumers. At first, it was thought that the answer could be found simply through cost-benefit analysis, but this led to a list which produced results which were unacceptable and was scrapped, mainly through poor costing and unreal estimates of the benefits. It seemed that the main determinant of the list was costs.

The commissioners tried to put each condition and the related treatments in priority order by another method: the question of costs was left for later consideration. The commission defined 17 categories of care and placed these categories in a priority ranking on the basis of value to society, value to the individual and being essential to a basic health care package. They then determined the net added value of particular conditions and associated treatments. The net added value was perceived as the difference in treating or not treating, judged by the chance of survival, the chance of cure and the chance of handicap. This was based on professional opinion. The commission then corrected this list considering such aspects as cost, public opinion, public values, medical opinion and their own judgements. It held 47 structured community meetings and 12 public hearings to elicit public opinion but most of those who chose to attend the meetings were health care providers.

A random telephone survey was undertaken to find how respondents valued a range of symptoms using Dr Kaplan's Quality of Well Being scale[101] with some additional items. This briefly covered mobility, physical activity and social activity. There were six degrees of functional impairment and 23 symptoms. The value assigned to each kind of limitation and the weights for each symptom were then subtracted from 1 which was assumed to be full health. Costs were assigned and checked with third party payers. Thus the services finally included were selected on the basis of the benefits which included the probability that a beneficial outcome would occur, the value that health care consumers placed on that outcome and how long the outcome would last. High rankings were inevitably given to prenatal care and adult and children's preventive services. Finally, the commissioners went though the list to see if it was an intuitively sensible ordering of conditions and treatments. Adjustments were made, mainly considering the public health impact of a condition/treatment and the cost. Less than 2 per cent remained in the position indicated by the formula.

Oregon needed a waiver from the requirements of the original Medicaid law to introduce the system. Thus the whole issue was reconsidered at the Federal level. At this stage the proposal fell foul of the lobby of the disabled. The Secretary of State objected that the telephone survey showed that Oregonians' rating of various health situations was based on the premise that the value of life of a person with a disability was less than the value of a person without a disability.[102] The list was then revised to eliminate the survey results and judgements about quality of life and placed greater weight on the judgement of the commissioners in assigning ranks. This far from objective plan for establishing priorities was finally approved in March 1993. One difficulty in gaining acceptance was that the basic package was to apply only to the poor not to all health insurance and even within Medicaid the elderly, disabled and blind and some others were to continue to have access to the previous full range of health benefits.

Norway's committee on priorities
A government committee reported in 1987. Four priority groups were listed with examples and a fifth category of interventions whose benefit was negligible or non-existent. The report, which was accepted by the Norwegian Parliament, highlighted the needs of the chronically ill and emphasized the need for preventive measures.

Sweden's medical priorities commission
A commission was set up by the government in 1992. Its first report emphasized the distinctions between efficient and inefficient care and between justified and unjustified care.[103] Ineffective care included:
- routine taking of specimens;
- mammography outside the age groups 50-70;
- tests for the exclusion of hypothetical risks;
- treatment of gastritis with anti-acid preparations;
- preventive treatment of high cholesterol blood levels with drugs except in hereditary forms or severe situations;
- continued treatment for an incurable disease after the treatment had proved to be inappropriate;
- terminal care which prolonged the process of dying without palliative effect;
- surgery for minor prostate disorders;
- several treatments for low back pain.

The commission rejected the idea of priorities being based on age, low birth weight or lifestyle, social or economic status. It listed the following priority groups for clinical activity:

Ia. Treatment of life-threatening acute diseases and diseases which, if left untreated, will lead to disability or premature death.
Ib. Treatment of severe chronic diseases. Palliative terminal care. Care of diseases which have led to a reduction of autonomy.
II. Habilitation/rehabilitation, together with provision of aids and individualized prevention which are not integral parts of care.
III. Treatment of less severe acute and chronic diseases.
IV. Care for reasons other than disease.
V. Self-care sufficient. Minor ailments.

In considering administrative priorities, the commission inserted a further category in II – population-based prevention and health screenings of documented cost-efficiency. The commission stressed that too little attention was given to Ib compared to II and III above.

USA – Proposed Health Security Act

President Clinton's Health Security bill is, at the time of writing, making its way through Congress along with several other bills on the subject of health care reform. Under the Health Security Act, all American citizens and legal residents would be guaranteed a comprehensive package of health benefits. The coverage guaranteed is generous and equals that provided by most major employers in the US. The package includes a wide range of clinical services and waives co-payments for basic preventive services such as pre-natal, well baby and well child checkups, physical examination for adults, immunizations, and major screening tests such as mammograms and Pap smears.[104]

Not everything is included in the basic package. Examples of excluded services are: services that are not medically necessary or appropriate; a private room in a hospital; adult spectacles and contact lenses; hearing aids; and cosmetic surgery. The precise services that will be excluded, as well as the definition of which are 'not medically necessary or appropriate' is not yet clear. Also unclear is how the basic benefit package will be defined at the federal level and how far it will be guaranteed over time. The states will have the freedom to interpret which services are appropriate or medically necessary.

New Zealand – Core Services Committee

In New Zealand an advisory committee called the National Advisory Committee on Core Health and Disability Support Services (or 'Core Services Committee') was set up in March 1992 which reports directly to the Minister for Health. The objectives of this committee were:

- to find an acceptable way of identifying which health care services should be publicly funded;
- to make the process of deciding what should be publicly funded more obvious;
- to recommend changes to that core of publicly funded services that reflect community values; and
- to define the terms of access – who gets which services within what time.[105]

When advising the Government, the Core Services Committee has to take into account the fact that resources are limited, and that 'ideally' everyone should have access to effective and affordable services without having to wait an unreasonable time for them. The Committee gives the Government advice annually on which services the state should pay for. If the government accepts this advice, then the four regional health authority purchasers are required (through a contract) to provide these services.

The Committee decides upon the services to be publicly funded using five key areas of information:

- the cost of the service;
- the effectiveness of the service;
- the current availability of the service;
- the responses of consultation with the public;

- an assessment of the impact of any recommended changes.

Assessing the effectiveness of services was done by reviewing published studies and by holding a series of consensus conferences. Sixteen conferences have now taken place and have focused on high volume or high cost services where the Committee believed there was a reasonable chance of reaching an applicable conclusion. Public consultation has taken various forms including self-administered postal questionnaires and public meetings.

The recommendations made by the Committee to the Government for 1993/4 had three themes:
- the broad range and volume of current services should continue,
- resources should shift gradually to reflect community priorities,
- services which are most effective should gradually receive more resources and waiting times for these services should be reduced.

Proposals for priorities in Spain

In February 1994, a working group of the Interterritorial Committee, which coordinates the regional health services of Spain, proposed a basic package of care to be provided under the National Health Service. It developed criteria for excluding services – the lack of sufficient evidence of clinical effectiveness, proven impact on life expectancy, increase in patient self-reliance or diminution of patient distress. On this basis it recommended the exclusion of in vitro fertilization, sex change interventions, aesthetic surgery, psychoanalysis, hypnosis and spa treatment. In the case of new treatments, the criteria proposed for inclusion were clinical effectiveness, the absence of cost-effective alternatives and the availability of technology and health professionals to provide the treatment.

Germany – essential health care

In Germany, in January 1993, the Federal Minister for Health requested the Advisory Council for the Concerted Action in Health Care to prepare an expert opinion on the development of social health insurance beyond the year 2000. Among the questions asked was 'Which benefits should remain an essential part of social health insurance after the year 2000? Are some statutory benefits no longer justified for reasons of health and social policy based on the principle of solidarity and subsidiarity? Should new benefits be provided by health insurance schemes?'

The Council reported in 1994 that in its opinion the cutting of legally anchored aspects of health care could only be carried out under the slogan 'rationalizing before rationing'. Whenever improvements in effectiveness and efficiency of medical care within the framework can be achieved, this should have priority over the limitation of benefits. It suggested medical, economic and socio-political criteria for categorizing benefits. Medical criteria could include the degree of life-saving and improvement in the quality of life involved in a particular treatment. Economic factors of importance are cost-effectiveness, insurability and price-elasticity of a particular treatment. Other economic criteria could be whether the cause of a particular treatment could be avoided by responsible personal behaviour and whether such behaviour represents a major financial risk. Examples of socio-political criteria could be cases of hardship and economic stress.[106]

Defining basic health care services in the Netherlands

The Dunning Committee,[107] was established by the Secretary of State responsible for health in the Netherlands. The main task of the committee was 'to examine how to put limits on new medical technologies and how to deal with the problems caused by scarcity of care, rationing of care, and the necessity of selection of patients for care'. This was at a time when publicly financed health care was to be extended to the whole population. The community approach to define health was used. The committee saw health as the ability to participate in society: thus inability to participate determined need and care made participation possible. The committee discussed the proposition that preference should be given to the young on the grounds that those who have reached the age of about 70 have had 'a fair innings' and rejected it. It saw this as conflicting with the universal right to self-determination. Each age has its own aims and these can vary greatly among individuals. There was no reason to assume that old people appreciated their lives less than young people, which would be ignored if one were to consider years of life instead of lives. Implicitly the committee rejected the counting of quality adjusted life years as a criterion for establishing priorities.

They recommended that each health care intervention should go through four different sieves. Was the care necessary, was it effective, was it efficient and should it be left to individual responsibility? They decided that necessary services fell into three groups. First, there were those services which could benefit every member of the community and which guaranteed normal functioning as a member of the community or protected existence as a member of the community. From a community point of view, these had the highest priority. These included facilities which guaranteed care for those members of society who could not care for themselves – nursing homes, psychogeriatrics and the care of the mentally handicapped. The second were facilities which again benefited all members of society but were principally aimed at restoring ability to participate in social activities; these included emergency medical services, care of premature babies, prevention of infectious diseases and centres for acute psychiatric patients. They also included services to prevent serious injury to health in the long run, such as care for people with serious chronic disorders, such as cancer, heart disease, sensory disorders and chronic psychiatric disease, but also preventive maternity care, care for children and newborns, vaccinations and identification of risks to health. In the third and last group were services, the necessity of which is determined by the severity of the disease and the number of persons with that disease.

Effectiveness was confined to confirmed and documented effectiveness. Efficiency would eliminate services of low effectiveness and high cost. Finally, the committee thought that limits could be set on solidarity when the costs were high and the chance of an effect was very slight: these could be left for individual payment.

The committee gave five helpful examples.

Excluded from basic care would be:

- in vitro fertilization on the grounds that one does not have a right to the ability to have children and that is not more than 30 per cent effective;
- homeopathic medicines on the grounds that their effectiveness had not been sufficiently demonstrated;
- dental care for adults on the grounds that this could be left to individual responsibility, given good dental care and prevention for the young;
- homes for the elderly on the grounds that nursing care of residents was essential care: housing costs and living costs should be an individual responsibility unless nursing assistance was needed and the individual was unable to meet the costs.

The committee decided to include in basic care:

- sporting injuries on the grounds that differences in life style did not provide a basis for exclusion.

These examples show, as the committee pointed out, that using the criteria was by no means easy. But the task of applying them has already begun and, as mentioned above, the Government has withdrawn homoeopathic drugs from the scope of health insurance.

Summary

All Member States need to cope with the important causes of ill health for which effective preventive, curative and rehabilitative care is available at tolerable cost. But where resources are limited, low effectiveness and high cost may exclude some types of care. In view of the limits to resources, effectiveness is a crucial principle. One of the main problems is the inadequacy of knowledge of what services are effective and what services are not. Thus one of the priorities is to identify gaps in present knowledge and fill those gaps. Research of this kind, which could be too expensive for some Member States to finance, could be affordable by the Union as a whole.

How far it would be acceptable to leave certain health needs to be paid for by the individual is clearly a matter for each Member State. Decisions will in part depend on ability to pay. Relevant here is whether there is an effective minimum income and the level at which it has been established. Decisions will also depend on the urgency for the provision of care. But it is arguable that those who want ineffective services should pay the whole cost of purchasing them.

The report of the Dunning Committee summarized above gives definitions and guidelines for health care, as distinct from wider health policy, which could be accepted as underlying the policies of Member States. In particular the definition of health could be adopted by the Union. 'Health is the ability to participate in society: thus inability to participate determines need and care makes participation possible'. Inability to participate in society can be a cause of social exclusion and income poverty. The aim in health policy should not just be to reduce premature mortality and extend life but to improve the quality of life. Services should be necessary, effective and efficient. Services that provide protection and care for the fragile, frail and disadvantaged should be given high priority, because they tend to be under-developed in many Member States.

7

Preventive Interventions and Health Promotion

This chapter starts with an examination of the links between curative services and health promotion, including preventive services. It then examines choices facing Member States concerning a series of specific interventions: immunization, antenatal care, family planning and breast and cervical screening. Finally, it considers policy choices in response to some of the major health challenges facing the population of the Union: tobacco and alcohol, HIV/AIDS, illicit drugs, and accidents.

Integration of preventive and curative services

In most Member States activities in prevention and health promotion are poorly integrated with curative services. Often, specific arrangements have been made by central or local government or through voluntary organizations to deliver services such as immunization and family planning. This is especially true in those systems based on social insurance although even in these systems, some Member States, such as the Netherlands, have managed to achieve relatively high levels of integration with curative services. All Member States have made specific arrangements to support health promotion activities, although their nature and the relationship with central government varies. In some Member States, such as Greece, Ireland and Italy there are health promotion units within Ministries of Health. In others, there are national bodies outside the Ministry, such as the Danish Health Education Council, the 'Comité Français d'Education Sanitaire' (see Box 7.1), the Dutch National Institute of Health Promotion and Education, and the British Health Education Authority. In Member States with national health services, health promotion functions are usually found at each level of the organization.

The following paragraphs examine some of the choices made by Member States in the fields of prevention and health promotion. They fall into three categories: specific interventions, such as immunization and screening; responses to major challenges to health, such as tobacco and AIDS; and strategies to meet the needs of disadvantaged groups.

Box 7.1: Comité Français d'Education Sanitaire

The committee was established in 1972 and works in association with the Ministry of Social Affairs. Its tasks are to study the health behaviour of the population and to develop, execute and coordinate programmes of health promotion at both the national and the local level. It publishes studies on health behaviour, publicity leaflets, a newsletter and several periodicals.

It has five departments:

- general affairs;
- strategic studies and documentation;
- communication, information and public relations;
- publications and dissemination;
- finance.

At the local level, regional and departmental committees for health education and inter-regional organizations participate in local campaigns and respond to the specific needs of particular regions or départements. In the past the committee has launched campaigns on tobacco, alcohol, vaccination and the excessive use of pharmaceuticals.

Specific interventions

Immunization

Childhood immunization against infectious disease is provided in all Member States although the spectrum of diseases covered (Table 7.1) and the arrangements for administering vaccine vary. All Member States include immunization against diphtheria, tetanus and polio. Most also include pertussis and measles, mumps; rubella and haemophilus influenza B is offered increasingly. Italy is the only Member State to offer immunization against hepatitis B as part of routine childhood immunization. Italy has a much higher incidence of this disease than many other parts of the European Union although, even here, it has been argued that this decision is not justified on economic grounds.[108] All vaccines are supplied free of charge in Belgium, Denmark, Greece, Italy, Netherlands, Portugal and the United Kingdom. In other Member States only some vaccines are provided free of charge.

Traditionally, in almost all Member States, immunization has been provided by several groups, including primary care doctors and separate clinics. The separate clinics have usually arisen because of the difficulty of ensuring that all primary care doctors undertook immunization. These have been established by various bodies.

For example, France has a network of state-run maternal and child health centres. In the Netherlands, municipalities run some clinics but others are managed by the voluntary Cross societies. In Belgium, a voluntary organization, the ONE, also plays a major role. In health systems based on social insurance, immunization is generally reimbursed by sickness funds. The United Kingdom is seeking to strengthen the role of general practitioners in this field. The approaches adopted to obtain high levels of coverage vary. In most Member States immunization is voluntary although highly encouraged.

Table 7.1: Availability of immunization

Country	BCG	DIP	TYP	PER	POL	MEA	MUM	RUB	HEP
Belgium	S	V	V	V	C	V	V	V	R
W.Germany	S	V	V	V	V	V	V	V	R
Denmark	R	V	V	V	V	V	V	V	R
Spain	V	V	V	V	V	V	V	V	A
France	C	C	C	V	C	V	V	V	R
Greece	C	C	C	C	C	C	V	V	R
Ireland	V	V	V	V	V	V	V	V	R
Italy	S	C	C	V	C	V	V	V	C
Luxembourg	V	V	V	V	V	V	V	V	R
Netherlands	S	V	V	V	V	V	V	V	R
Portugal	V	C	C	C	C	V	V	V	R
United Kingdom	V	V	V	V	V	V	V	V	R

V – voluntary
C – compulsory
S – compulsory for some age groups or special conditions
R – for those at risk only
A – adolescents in some autonomous regions

Source: Protection of Public Health by Vaccination, STOA Project, European Parliament, 1993.

The take up of immunization varies considerably between Member States (see Table 7.2). By comparing experiences it should be possible to identify the factors leading to success.

Table 7.2: Percentage of children immunized (1991)

Country	Diphtheria	Tetanus	Pertussis	Measles	Polio
Belgium	94.2	94.2	94.2	66.6	99.5
Germany	90.0 90.0*	90.0*	60.0 70.0*	70.0 70.0*	90.1 99.0*
Denmark	97.0 98.0*	97.0 98.0*	94.0 93.0*	86.0 85.0*	97.0 98.0*
Spain	86.0 84.0*	86.0 84.0*	86.0 84.0*	88.0 83.0*	88.0 85.0*
France	92.0	92.0	89.0 84.0*	77.0 76.0*	92.0 99.5*
Greece	90.0	90.0	54.0***	76.0[1]	77.0
Ireland	65[1]	65.0[1]	65.0[1]	78.0[2]	63.0
Italy	95.0*	95.0*	40.0*	50.0*	98.0*
Luxembourg	90.0[1]	90.0[1]	90.0[1]	80.0	90.0[1]
Netherlands	97.0*	97.0*	97.0*	94.0*	97.0*
Portugal	96.0 92.4*	96.0 94.4*	95.4 94.1*	96.4 95.2*	94.9 93.0*
UK	90.0	90.0	90.0	89.0[1]	95.0

*   1992   [1]   1990
***   1985   [2]   1989

Source: WHO Health for All Data-Base, except for Ireland and Spain where new figures have been provided by the Ministries of Health.

Ante-natal care

High quality ante-natal care is thought to be one factor in reducing the frequency of low birth weight and hence perinatal mortality, although the evidence is conflicting.[109,110,111] In addition, it is increasingly seen as a mechanism for early detection of foetal abnormalities, thus giving mothers the choice about whether to continue with the pregnancy. Ante-natal care is regarded as a priority in all Member States but the pattern of delivery of services varies widely. A few Member States, such as Denmark, Ireland, the Netherlands, and the United Kingdom, have relatively integrated services involving primary care doctors, midwives and hospital doctors. In some Member States, services are provided in parallel by two or more organizations. For example, in France, services are available from primary care doctors, where payment is required but is reimbursed, or free at maternal and child health services. In all Member States, attendance is voluntary but France makes attendance a prerequisite for payment of child benefit. Similarly, in Luxembourg, ante-natal services are provided free of charge by primary care doctors. Although these services are not compulsory, patients receive financial incentives to use them.

Family planning
Unplanned pregnancies are an important public health issue because of their social consequences, especially among young women. Teenage pregnancies vary widely among Member States, with the highest levels in the United Kingdom. In many Member States, family planning is available from primary care doctors or in separate clinics. The existence of separate clinics in some countries is part of an official policy to encourage adolescents to attend, as they might otherwise be reluctant to visit their family doctor. Some such clinics are run by voluntary bodies such as the Brook clinics in the United Kingdom, the 'Rutgers Stichting' in the Netherlands, the National Family Planning Association in Luxembourg or Pro-Familia in Germany. In some Member States, such as Denmark, contraceptives must be paid for. In others, they are partly (e.g. Belgium) or completely (United Kingdom) covered by the health service or sickness funds. In Germany, oral contraceptives are free for the under 21s.

Breast cancer screening
Breast cancer is the leading cause of death among women in the Union aged between 35 and 64. There is now evidence from randomized controlled trials that well organized mammography programmes can bring about a reduction in mortality from breast cancer.[112,113] Screening is available on request in all Member States but only a few have systematic programmes. The only four Member States with national programmes involving population registers, systematic invitations, and integrated follow-up are Germany, Luxembourg, the Netherlands and the United Kingdom (see Boxes 7.2 and 7.3). In Luxembourg, breast cancer screening is offered free of charge to all women aged between 50 and 64 years. From its implementation in 1992, 55 per cent of the target population has been screened.

Some other Member States have introduced screening programmes as either experimental programmes or as local initiatives, such as an experimental breast screening programme in 21 French Départements which will extended to the whole of France in 1997. There are also programmes in the city of Copenhagen, in Liege and Brabant in Belgium, in North Dublin, Monaghan and Cavan in Ireland, in the central region in Portugal (Coimbra), in Florence in Italy and in the Spanish region of Navarre. The French programme will be extended throughout the country during 1994 to 1998. In several Member States, the absence of population-based registers with details of age is an obstacle to the introduction of systematic screening programmes. In some of these, opportunistic screening is available. (See Box 7.4).

Box 7.2: Breast cancer screening programme in the Netherlands

The breast screening programme arose from two non-experimental studies undertaken in Utrecht and Nijmegen in 1974/75. The results were published in 1984 and the Health Secretary decided to extend them nationally. In 1987 the Health Insurance Executive Board was requested to implement this, with a programme of two-yearly screening for women aged 50 to 69. It established a national coordinating committee that produced guidelines for quality assurance, subsequently endorsed by the relevant professional bodies. A national reference centre was established, with responsibility for training those involved in the programme as well as for quality assurance. Subsequently an economic evaluation was undertaken that indicated that the programme had the potential to save 700 lives per year, at DFl 8000 per life saved. In 1993 a mid-term review was undertaken that supported continuation of the programme. The programme should be implemented fully by the end of 1994. Uptake is currently approximately 80 per cent. It is funded by the Exceptional Medical Expenses Act and is provided free to patients.

Box 7.3: Breast cancer screening programme in the United Kingdom

The breast screening programme was introduced in 1987 following a review of evidence by an expert panel (Forrest Report). It is nationally coordinated within the National Health Service, in line with policy set by the Department of Health. The National Coordinator is responsible for coordinating quality assurance, training, education, equipment and publicity and circulating guidance on good practice. Breast screening services are purchased by District Health Authorities on behalf of their populations. There are no specific financial incentives to providers except via the contracting mechanism to provide a high quality service. Breast screening is provided free to patients. All women aged 50-64 should receive an invitation for screening and screening should be made available to women aged 65 and over on request. Nationally, 66 of the 77 planned centres opened by the target date of 31 March 1990, but the delay in the opening of the remainder postponed the target of inviting all eligible women for screening by 1992. The national average of uptake rates of screening from first (prevalent) and subsequent rounds combined for women aged 50 and over is 71.3 per cent.

Screening for cervical cancer

There is evidence that systematic screening for cervical cancer can be effective in reducing mortality.[114] It should, however, be undertaken within well organized population-based screening programmes with high quality cytological support.[115] Systematic national population-based programmes are available in Germany, Luxembourg, the Netherlands and the United Kingdom. Several local programmes are also in existence, such as in some Danish counties, and in a programme managed by the Greek Oncological Society that provides a service in rural parts of the country. There are programmes in three French departments and in a defined population in the Greater Dublin area. Local health services in Portugal have tried to develop pilot programmes.

Box 7.4: The cancer screening programme in Western Germany

The cancer screening programme started in 1971 when the Bundestag adopted a law which entitled all members of the health insurance system to take advantage of screening programmes at yearly intervals. For cancer screening (beginning at the age of 45) the following were chosen:

- breast cancer
- cervical cancer
- colorectal cancer
- prostate cancer
- skin cancer.

In 1982, the Federal Board of Doctors and the governmental authorities tried to establish a sound base for improving this programme. As a result, the age of entry to the programme was changed (women were permitted to have a breast inspection from the age of 30) and the documentation on screening was improved.

The German practice of using mammography in all problematic cases and for risk groups is undergoing a scientific review.

The training of most of the GPs as well as of the radiologists cannot be regarded as sufficient if the programme is extended. Nevertheless, provisions were made to implement mammography in terms of a country wide test and not only to improve the efficiency of the programme but also to train doctors in this field. Another problem is the rather low participation rate.

With the codification of the Vth volume of the Social Law Book (SGB V) in 1989 which replaces the old Reichsversicherungsordnung two additional elements have been added to the screening programme.

a) Cancer screening is now combined with a general screening programme which includes checks on risk factors (cholesterol, blood pressure, renal functions, diabetes etc.) and the doctors advise their patients on how to avoid major health risks (overweight, tobacco and alcohol abuse etc.) by changing behaviour.

b) The health insurers are required to provide training courses for their members to acquire a more healthy lifestyle. These new elements were designed to attract more GPs to participate actively in this programme.

An evaluation will be made in 1995 to review the efficiency of this new preventive programme.

Responses to major challenges to health

The following paragraphs consider examples of the ways in which Member States have tackled some of the major threats to health, as identified in Chapter 1 of this report: tobacco and alcohol consumption, HIV/AIDS, illicit drugs, and accidents.

Tobacco

As shown above, levels of smoking vary widely among Member States. So do strategies to reduce them. Three principal approaches have been adopted, fiscal, legislative, and educational. Most Member States have high levels of taxation on tobacco but only a few, such as France and the United Kingdom, have stated explicitly that this is for health reasons. In France, between 1950 and 1989, the real price of tobacco in terms of levels of income fell and the volume of consumption increased each year. In the United Kingdom, the real price has gone up and down in different periods and consumption has responded precisely in the reverse direction. The fiscal policies adopted in France and the United Kingdom have the publicly stated objective of decreasing consumption rather than simply raising revenue. The Greek government has proposed a hypothecated tax on tobacco that would provide support for the health system.

The taxes on cigarettes in ECUs are shown in Table 7.3. The highest taxes are in Germany, Ireland and the United Kingdom. The taxes are remarkably low in Luxembourg, considering its standard of living. In some countries rolled tobacco bears lower taxation than manufactured cigarettes with the result that more tobacco is consumed in this form. For example, the market share of rolled tobacco is 49 per cent in the Netherlands. An indication of the extent to which tobacco prices have been changing is shown in the Table as the ratio of the price of tobacco to the consumer price index (1985 = 100). It should, however, be noted that two Member States have removed tobacco from the retail price index – Luxembourg in 1990 and Belgium in 1991. The weight it has in the consumer price index varies from 1.1 per cent in Belgium to 3.3 per cent in Ireland. Most Member States have also introduced legislation restricting tobacco advertising and the places that smoking can take place. The United Kingdom has sought voluntary agreements rather than using legislation, although a report by the British Department of Health's chief economic advisor has reviewed the evidence and concluded that a legal ban on advertising would be beneficial. Most Member States also have some educational programmes but their extent and nature vary considerably. A recent review concluded that increased taxation, banning tobacco advertising, and encouraging medical personnel and leading figures to take leadership roles were the most effective and cheapest strategies.[116] However the first two of these also provoke the strongest resistance from the tobacco industry.

Table 7.3: Tobacco taxation and tobacco pricing

Member State	Tax per 1000 cigarettes+ in ECU 1992	Index of tobacco/consumer price index 1985=100
Belgium	68.8	113.3**
Germany	146.6	106.8*
Denmark	83.8	93.0**
Spain	16.6	102.6***
France	61.0	113.5**
Greece	34.7	133.1*
Luxembourg	48.4	106.7*
Italy	55.0	108.9*
Ireland	112.9	108.7**
Netherlands	62.3	102.1**
Portugal	45.1	n/a
United Kingdom	117.8	100.7*

+ most popular brand *1990, **1989, ***1988

Source: The European Commission (unpublished data).

Alcohol

In Table 7.4 is shown the consumption of alcohol per head in 1990. The highest consumption was in France and the lowest in the United Kingdom with the exception of Greece for which no figures for spirits' consumption are available. There has been a considerable trend downward in France, Italy and Spain. But there has been a substantial upward trend in Denmark, Netherlands and the United Kingdom and to a lesser extent in Luxembourg.

Health promotion activities focus on both the direct effects of alcohol and on driving after drinking alcohol. Typically the latter programmes are managed by Ministries of Transport although the Netherlands has a Traffic Safety Foundation ('Velig Verkeer Nederland') that undertakes extensive educational activities. Germany, similarly, has the 'Verkehrssicherheitsrat'. Ireland is developing a national alcohol strategy and targets for reducing alcohol consumption are contained within the cardiovascular disease key area of the British 'Health of the Nation' strategy. Strategies to reduce alcohol consumption include increasing the cost (although this is threatened in some countries by proposals to harmonize taxes), education and restrictions on access. Strategies need to take into account the diverse roles which alcohol plays in social life in different Member States.

Table 7.4: Trends in alcohol consumption

Member State	Consumption Litres per head 1990	Increase (+) Decrease (-) 1970-90
Belgium	9.9	+ 11.1
W. Germany	10.6	+2.6
Denmark	9.9	+45.0
Spain	10.8	-7.1
France	12.7	-21.9
Greece	5.9*	+11.4
Luxembourg	12.2	+22.0
Italy	8.7	-36.8
Ireland	7.2	+21.3
Netherlands	8.2	+46.4
Portugal	9.8	-1.5
United Kingdom	7.6	+44.2

*wine and beer only

Source: World Drink Trends, 1992 Edition.

AIDS

As shown in Chapter 1, the extent of HIV infection and AIDS varies widely among Member States as does the pattern of transmission. In some parts of Member States, such as England, spread has been predominantly through homosexual contact whereas in Spain and Italy, intravenous drug abuse has been the commonest vehicle for infection. There are also important variations within Member States both in incidence, with higher levels typically in urban rather than rural areas, and in the mode of transmission. For example, in Scotland, intravenous drug abuse has been the most important mode of transmission.

The policies adopted by Member States reflect the differences in the scale of the challenge which they face, as well as the context within which policies are developed. Many Member States have established high level committees or organizations to bring together relevant groups. For example, the United Kingdom established an inter-ministerial committee. Ireland has a national AIDS strategy committee, and France has established the 'Agence Nationale de Lutte contre le SIDA' (see Box 7.5). The government also finances several projects initiated by the AIDES Federation, a non-profit organization which has developed 31 regional committees responsible for reception and support centres. As in France, Portugal has a 'Comissao Nacional de Luta contra o SIDA'.

Box 7.5: HIV/AIDS policy in France

Public awareness of HIV/AIDS is high in France, partly as a result of lobbying by non-profit organizations, such as AIDES and Act-Up, and concerns about contamination of blood products. A review of HIV/AIDS policy has been prepared by Professor Luc Montagnier, the discoverer of the virus, entitled 'AIDS and French Society'. The main recommendations, accepted by the government, include the establishment of an inter-ministerial committee chaired by the Prime Minister and mechanisms for co-ordination of activities at local level.

In Belgium a system of paying for home care of AIDS patients has been developed as shown in Box 7.6.

Box 7.6: Home care for AIDS patients in Belgium

A system of reimbursing home care for AIDS patients in Belgium was announced in January 1994. The scheme is based on the Saint Pierre hospital which treats about half the AIDS patients needing medical care in Belgium. The hospital will be reimbursed at the rate of BFr 4000 for up to ten home visits in the course of three months. There will be no co-payment. This compares with the cost of in-patient care which is BFr 20 000 per day. The co-payment for this is BFr 1000 per day. The scheme may be extended to other hospitals.

The strategies adopted by Member States vary considerably. They reflect the diversity of methods of transmission and include educational programmes aimed at the promotion of safe sex and the reduction of needle-sharing by drug addicts, improved access to items such as condoms and needle exchange programmes, screening of blood products, and training of health professionals.

Illicit drugs

Action on illicit drugs, both at the levels of the Union and Member States, are often led by interior and justice departments. Involvement by health agencies is often closely linked to strategies on HIV/AIDS because of the importance of needle-sharing as a method of HIV transmission. Strategies vary widely among Member States.[117] All are signatories to the 1961 United Nations convention on the control of narcotics and, as a result, all have made possession of certain drugs an offence. There are, however, differences in the degree to which the laws are enforced, with some Member States placing less emphasis on the possession of small quantities of drugs such as cannabis for personal use.

Policies to treat addiction include the use of methadone substitution, either for short term use or maintenance, and residential or community rehabilitation programmes. The choice of strategy and the level of provision vary widely among Member States. Methadone substitution is used extensively in Denmark, the United Kingdom and the Netherlands but rarely in France or Greece.[118] Despite the diversity and the scope for comparative studies, relatively little is known about the effectiveness of different policies. This presents a major challenge for the European Monitoring Centre for Drugs and Drug Addiction, newly established in Portugal.

Motor vehicle accidents

Policies to reduce deaths from motor vehicle accidents typically are managed by Ministries of Transport. The principal strategies used are educational programmes, improvements in vehicular safety, traffic calming schemes, and enforcement of speed limits. The extent to which different approaches have been adopted varies considerably among Member States, as do their results. In some Member States, there is a strong argument in favour of implementing existing policies more widely. For example, educational programmes, such as that developed in the Netherlands by the Traffic Safety Foundation ('Veilig Verkeer Nederland'), have only been implemented in a few other Member States, despite impressive results. In other cases, there is still a debate about the relative effectiveness of different strategies. For example, it has been proposed that increasing vehicular safety encourages car drivers to take greater risks, with resulting adverse consequences for pedestrians. In addition, the motor industry has opposed EU proposals to improve vehicle safety standards on the basis of cost and competitiveness.

Can preventive action save curative costs?

Effective preventive interventions have clear benefits in terms of the reductions in human suffering that they bring about. They are also seen by some as a means of reducing health care costs. This belief probably comes from historical experience. One cannot, however, generalize from one example to another. For example, the sharp drop in the incidence and mortality of infectious diseases from the nineteenth century can be attributed to safe water, sanitation, improved nutrition, personal hygiene and much later to the development and widespread use of more and more effective immunizing agents. The saving in the use of hospital beds with the final world eradication of smallpox and the rareness of cases of typhoid, cholera, typhus, diphtheria, poliomyelitis, and tuberculosis was immense and greatly exceeded the cost of the early immunization campaigns. The fact that the saved hospital beds were used for other cases, as curative knowledge developed, does not take away from this achievement. This highlights an important methodological problem in answering this question. As costs are incurred now and benefits realized later, the analysis is highly sensitive to the choice of time period or discount rate used.

Once the incidence of infectious diseases is brought down to low levels by routine immunization of a large proportion of children, the question of the adverse side effects on a small minority becomes relevant. It was calculated after the United States had no smallpox cases for twenty years that vaccination was causing by the late 1960s seven or eight deaths a year, hundreds of complications, about 200 of them requiring admission to hospital, and thousands of mild reactions.[119] From a short term point of view prevention was costing more than cure. At that stage the alternative of quarantine was considered with vaccination of health workers, military recruits and travellers to countries where small pox was endemic. This policy was finally adopted in 1971.

The answers obtained will also depend on whether the costs measured are those to health services or also include those to society in general. It was shown in a calculation for 1963-8 in the United States that the total medical care cost of vaccination was greater than not vaccinating. The savings measured came from the reduction in the number of persons needing care because of brain damage.[120] However, it by no means follows that immunization is not a good investment. The disease caused substantial suffering to children and concern for their parents, both difficult to value.

The case of rubella is more problematic. The disease is normally mild but can cause serious deformities in a pregnant woman's unborn child. If the proportion of the population vaccinated falls below 70 per cent, it is suggested that the reservoir of vulnerable people can mean that the syndrome runs in cycles – at times above the level that would have occurred without vaccination as, without it, most women are naturally immune by the time they reach adulthood.[121] In addition the vaccine does cause acute neurological conditions in the range of one disorder per 44 000 to 360 000 vaccinations.[122] Thus, in the United Kingdom, only girls aged 11-13 are the target for immunization.

The case of influenza is even more complex as the disease changes in cycles of 5-7 years so that old vaccines soon become no longer protective. There is certainly a case for using it for high risk groups such as the elderly, where a mild case of influenza can be life-threatening.[123] The Office of Technology Assessment in the United States estimated that, for pneumococcal pneumonia, vaccines could reduce medical costs for those 45 and older but not for younger people.[124]

As the number of premature deaths have declined, those that remain are largely the consequences of the interrelated factors of lifestyle and environment. The difficulty is to calculate what it would cost to persuade people to adopt healthy life styles. For example, virtually everyone knows that smoking has high health risks and that alcohol in excess is health-damaging. But changes in knowledge do not necessarily lead to changes in attitudes or practice. It can be shown in small studies that counselling by health workers can be effective. General practitioners who offered patients who smoked advice on stopping, gave them a leaflet and warned that they would be followed up, achieved a 5.1 per cent cessation rate after one year, compared to 0.3 per cent for controls who were only asked if they smoked or not.[125] Nurses can be even more effective: in one study 17 per cent of the experimental group had given up smoking after a year compared with 8.3 per cent of controls.[126] But it is not possible to generalize from such studies. Smoking is on the decrease. Is this simply due to higher taxation? What part has health education played, warnings on cigarette packets and attention to the question in the media? Alcohol consumption is on the increase in the United Kingdom despite similar warnings about the dangers of consuming it in excess. Is this because the price in real terms has come down? There is evidence from 15 different trials that brief medical consultations consisting of assessment of intake and provision of information and advice can reduce alcohol consumption by 20 per cent at a cost of about 30 ECUs[127] per consultation.

It is extremely difficult to work out whether exercise saves treatment costs. Exercise is not costless depending on the form it takes. Even running can cause costs in injuries arising from it and needs new shoes and clothes: it certainly takes considerable time to do it several times a week. And there is no proven evidence from randomized controlled trials that non-sedentary people who do not have heart disease can reduce their risks by exercise. The studies done so far compare active people with sedentary people and considerable uncertainty remains about the amount and kind of exercise needed to achieve the benefits shown in studies of heart disease and other conditions. And if exercise is beneficial which seems likely, it is not known at what cost to whom more people can be persuaded to take it.

There is, however, evidence from 28 separate studies in the United States that health promotion at the workplace can reduce health care costs. The savings are generally three or more times greater than the cost of the programme.[128] Many of them have used randomized or parallel control groups in similar work places, where there is no primary health care system.

It is notoriously difficult to document savings in costs from screening programmes for the early detection of disease.[129] The cost of screening plus the cost of treating those detected before there are symptoms can be much higher than that of treating those who develop symptoms.[130] The question of whether screening for high blood pressure saves treatment costs is very difficult to answer simply because of the number of variables which have to be estimated. It depends on the prevalence of high blood pressure, the cut off point that is used for 'high' and the accuracy of screening tests which produce 50 per cent of false positives at the first test. It also depends on the willingness of people to persist with a treatment which has unpleasant side effects, the incidence of the disease and how successfully the disease, if it develops, can be treated and at what cost.[131] Nevertheless, it has been boldly estimated for the United Kingdom that the better control of hypertension saved the costs of hospitals of £205 million in 1985 at a cost of £185 million for all antihypertensives at manufacturer's prices.[132] But drugs are only part of the costs of screening programmes.

The main potential savings in treatment costs of preventive measures is in the form of reduced hospital use – either by making it possible to avoid admission or making surgery unnecessary. There may also be less visits to doctors, tests and drugs. Now hospital budgets are restricted in nearly all Member States and, in many, there are waiting lists for admission, if one patient is discharged earlier, another is admitted. If one patient is not admitted, another may be admitted instead with no saving in cost. Thus savings could turn out to be theoretical rather than actual. But this is true of many other measures to increase efficiency.

While prevention has great potential, it has costs and risks. Risks often emerge after widespread application. And if older peoples' lives are saved from one condition, they are likely to need medical care for another later on. It cannot be assumed that prevention is cheaper than cure in every case. Each option needs to be considered on its merits. In some cases cure may be cheaper than prevention. Often the question is what mix of cure and prevention is best and how to direct preventive programmes towards those at greatest risk. Good health has a value of its own and is worth paying for. Prevention does not necessarily offer a way of reducing curative medical costs despite the increased health benefits.

Summary

This brief review has demonstrated the great diversity in the policies developed by Member States in the fields of prevention and health promotion and has given some indication of the differences in their effects. Although the magnitude of different public health challenges varies among Member States, many of these challenges are common to all. This diversity provides a valuable natural laboratory to compare the impact of differing policies. To some extent this is utilized in projects under the auspices of the Europe against Cancer, Europe against AIDS, and BIOMED I programmes, although further valuable comparisons could be made.

Increasing mobility of people, goods and services means that many of the challenges to public health in Europe require a response at the level of the Union. Obvious examples include harmonization of fiscal policies with regard to alcohol and tobacco, coordination of advertising policies, and improvements in safety standards for vehicles and other consumer goods.

There is considerable potential for effective preventive strategies to bring about substantial improvements in both the length and quality of life of the population of Europe. Such policies should not, however, be seen as a means of cost containment.

8

Migrants and Ethnic Minorities

Health needs of migrants

The breaking down of borders in Europe is expected to lead to a continuing increase in the number of migrants within the Union. Movement is both between Member States within the Union and from other countries. There is a long tradition of movement between certain Member States, such as Ireland and the United Kingdom, but this is increasing as a result of the single market. One group that has been moving between European countries for centuries is the Romany or gypsy population. They have obvious difficulties in access to health services. Recent estimates of their numbers in certain Member States are given in Table 8.1.

Table 8.1: Estimates of the gypsy population in certain Member States

Country	Estimated number
Belgium	150000
Germany	120000
Spain	690000
France	250000
Greece	150000
Italy	90000
United Kingdom	110000

Source: Europ, Winter 1994.

Movement into the Union from other countries has traditionally involved people from other parts of Southern Europe, such as Turkey, or from countries in Asia, Africa, and Latin America, with patterns reflecting linguistic and colonial links. But much of immigration into Denmark is from other Nordic countries. Between 1945 and 1990 there has been very little movement from the countries of central and eastern Europe, but this is now increasing rapidly. The overall levels of migrant populations in Member States is shown in Table 8.2, and their continent of origin is shown in Table 8.3, although these summary statistics obscure the enormous diversity in these populations.

Table 8.2: Total population of third country nationals, and the refugee population legally resident in Member States (1000s)

Member State	1986			1992			
	Total pop.	Non-EU nat.	%	Total pop.	Non-EU nat.	%	Refugee pop.
Belgium	9858.9	308.4	3.13	10022.0	367.9	3.67	24300
Germany	61020.5	3022.3	4.95	64484.8	4,395.0	6.82	827100
Denmark	5116.3	91.1	1.78	5162.1	141.1	2.73	58300
Spain	38542.1	121.9	0.32	39055.9	202.4	0.52	9700
France	53173.9	2285.7	4.30	56163.2	2,357.7	4.14	182600
Greece	9949.1	185.3	1.86	10120.0	174.9	1.73	8500
Ireland	3541.3	17.9	0.51	3524.0	–	–	200
Italy	57202.4	–	–	56757.0	425.9	0.75	12400
Luxembourg	367.2	–	–	389.8	13.9	3.56	2200
Netherlands	14529.4	391.0	2.69	15129.2	557.4	3.68	26900
Portugal	10185.0	59.0	0.58	9846.0	83.9	0.85	1800
UK	55913.6	1052.1	1.88	56960.3	1,207.2	2.12	100000

Source: a) EUROSTAT (1994), unpublished data; b) United Nations High Commissioner for Refugees (1993), *The State of the World's Refugees*, UNCHR, Penguin Books.

Migrant populations have specific health needs for several reasons. Their patterns of disease are often different from those seen in the indigenous population.

This may be because of genetic differences, such as sickle cell disease, primarily seen among those of African origin and thalassaemia, primarily seen among those of Southern European origin. Genetic factors may also be involved in a complex interplay with environmental factors, such as the increased prevalence of diabetes mellitus in south Asians. Migrants are often on the margins of society and, thus, at increased risk of the diseases associated with poverty. Visits to families remaining in developing countries may expose them to diseases which are relatively uncommon in Europe, such as tuberculosis and diphtheria. Unfortunately, these populations are often doubly disadvantaged as, despite an increased burden of disease, they often have reduced access to preventive measures and to health services for linguistic, financial, and other factors. Access is especially problematic for clandestine migrants who may avoid formal care because of the perceived risk of deportation. For these reasons, it is necessary to ensure that preventive and curative services are designed explicitly to meet the needs of migrant populations.

Table 8.3: Population by citizenship on 1 January 1991 – total figures for Europe/Africa/America/Asia

	Europe (non-EU)	Africa	America	Asia
Belgium	107227	181284	19348	22205
Germany	3016091	197974	144633	513420
Denmark	71271	7063	7920	38247
Greece	40213	19117	28647	36130
Spain	33336	39875	98438	36130
France	349594	1633142	72758	226956
Ireland	1800	–	7600	–
Italy	118024	238565	128362	140279
Luxembourg	5132	1724	1836	1612
Netherlands	234210	186225	42153	52956
Portugal	2646	45255	26369	4154
United Kingdom	149000	148000	221000	453000
EU	4128544	2698224	799064	1525089

Source: EUROSTAT (1994), unpublished data.

Services for migrants and ethnic minorities

Member States appear to vary considerably in the extent to which they have made specific provision for the needs of migrants and ethnic minorities. In part, this is because the extent of migration to different Member States has varied. For example, there has been very little immigration to Ireland and the origin of migrants varies considerably, reflecting geography and historical colonial connections, with concentrations of people from Turkey and Central and Eastern Europe in Germany and the Netherlands, from North Africa in France, from Surinam in the Netherlands, and from the Caribbean and the Indian sub-continent in the United Kingdom. Mass migration may emerge from the political changes in the former USSR. This could have major implications for the health of the Union's population. For example, hepatitis B is endemic in the Commonwealth of Independent Sates (CIS): incidence of it increased from 13.5 to 42.0 per 100 000 between 1974 and 1987.[133]

There are also differences in the way in which migrants are viewed in different countries. For example, although there has been extensive migration from Ireland to the United Kingdom, some official reports on ethnic minorities have excluded them. Member States also vary in the extent to which ethnic minorities have been assimilated with the native population, reflecting various factors including race, religion and the passage of generations. Furthermore, because of the uneven distribution of migrants in each country, this has more often stimulated local rather than national initiatives. Unfortunately, there is still relatively little information collected in a systematic way as to how Member States are responding to this challenge. A major problem is the difficulty in knowing how many people are involved, partly because of a lack of explicit and meaningful definitions, especially with regard to naturalized and second generation migrants, and partly because of the extent of clandestine migration and the movement of gypsies across frontiers. One Member State (the United Kingdom) includes a question in the census seeking respondents' own perceptions on their ethnicity, overcoming problems related to second generation migrants. From April 1993, the British health service has included ethnic monitoring to document the delivery of health services to ethnic communities in each health district. The aim is to raise basic questions about the way in which services are provided, policies developed and priorities established.

Six per cent of the Dutch population consists of minorities. They include migrant workers from countries surrounding the Mediterranean sea, migrants from former Dutch colonies, invited refugees and asylum seekers. In 1992, there were about 40 000 newcomers. There is a department of refugees, minorities and asylum seekers in the Ministry of Welfare, Health and Culture which supervises the arrangements for their welfare. Both asylum seekers and invited refugees are received in the central reception centres where they are given food, clothing etc. and their insurance is paid for them while they are introduced to Dutch society and culture. After the reception period, it is the responsibility of the municipalities to make housing available, pay allowances to them and provide legal and health insurance.

There is a special Bureau for Health Education for Foreigners in the Netherlands. A number of voluntary bodies are subsidized by the government which organize support groups of volunteers. In Flanders, intercultural workers in health care are being appointed to improve communication between health workers and ethnic minorities.

In Italy, there are no special programmes for immigrants, but under a law of 1990 immigrants are granted special rights such as to be protected under social security if they have a job, to register with the unemployment office and the local registry office with means that they have the right to use the National Health Service. But these rights are often not used as they must ask for registration with the health service and are not well informed about the procedures. As a result, they tend to use the emergency services rather than general practitioners.

In many countries the voluntary sector plays an important role, such as 'Médecins du Monde' in France and Spain. In the latter 'Medicos del Mundo' have set up primary health and social centres for illegal immigrants in four cities – Madrid, Bilbao, Valencia and Seville. These centres are staffed by volunteers and have also mobile units to facilitate access. Also, in Spain, the 'Medicos sin Fronteras' have started a programme to help illegal immigrants in the suburbs of Barcelona with the aim of integrating this population into the health and social services. Provision for migrants and ethnic minorities in Germany, France and the United Kingdom is shown in Boxes 8.1, 8.2 and 8.3.

As pointed out earlier, migrants have specific health needs that require specific responses. There is relatively little publicly available material on how these needs are identified and met in many Member States and it appears that they are often not regarded as a priority. The research that has been done indicates that it is insufficient to assume that simply making services available ensures that they will be used.

Box 8.1: The situation of ethnic minorities in German health care

There are no special programmes catering for ethnic minorities in Germany. For permanent residents, the insurance benefits are the same for all groups, regardless of nationality. However, for non-permanent residents (like asylum-seekers or refugees), there is a small but important difference: working family members are insured just like their German colleagues, but family members are not (though they are for permanent residents). In case of the illness of family members, treatment must be covered privately, if the earner's wage is high enough; otherwise, social security steps in. Some counties (Kreise) and towns have agreed to pay for private bulk insurance for these groups of people. These are local initiatives inspired by the fact that social security is paid for by the counties/towns themselves.

A different problem is caused by language difficulties and cultural differences in behaviour. There is no formal legislation or programme to cope with this. Rather, the concept of self-government implies that this should be tackled locally as the need arises. In particular, in areas with a high percentage of foreign native speakers, the insurance funds employ fluent speakers of the main foreign languages to cater for these groups. Often, this means employing second-generation immigrants or foreign workers. Examples include Turkish employees in parts of Berlin or Italians in Cologne. The same holds for many hospitals. Also, there are foreign nationality doctors to be found in these areas (though not by any specific programme of settlement). In addition, nearly all booklets, leaflets and forms used in health services are available in the major foreign languages spoken in Germany.

With respect to cultural diversity, there is a hard rule that states that the patient has to collaborate with the medical professional in order to be treated and to receive sick benefits etc. From this it might be deduced that people denying certain forms of treatment (e.g., for religious or cultural reasons) can be sanctioned. In practice, this is not applied. Office-based doctors and hospitals alike are aware of these potential problems and try to overcome them by education and by not forcing any form of treatment. In other cases – e.g. for Islamic women not wanting to be treated by male doctors, there are usually female doctors available. Again, the solutions are not based on legislation but on local initiative.

Box 8.2: Health care for foreigners and migrants in France

By virtue of the law introduced in 1993 (24/8/93), access to social security and social aid for foreigners residing in France has been restricted by the modification of the entitlement prerequisites. Foreign workers have to possess a permanent permit of residence or proof that they have applied for renewal of their permit to stay in order to be entitled to compulsory and supplementary insurance. The only exceptions are foreign prisoners who do not have to fulfil the above criteria.

All foreigners entitled to social security benefit have a right to all the cash benefits of sickness insurance for care provided in France (reimbursement of medical fees, pharmaceuticals, hospitalization fees etc.). Those who are not entitled to social insurance will not be entitled to any sickness insurance benefit. If for any reason someone stops being entitled he/she will continue to benefit from the social security system for one year.

Medical aid is provided independently of a permanent permit of residence in cases in which care was provided by a health institution (i.e. hospital, medical aid); it also covers all prescriptions written on such occasions as well as those for out-patient care following hospitalization.

Domiciliary medical care is also subject to a permanent permit of residence or uninterrupted stay in metropolitan France for a minimum of 3 years. This automatically excludes those suffering from chronic and serious diseases (AIDS, cancer, tuberculosis) who either opt for hospitalization or wish to die at home with all the risks which this would involve for themselves and their families.

Social security centre of migrant workers
(Centre de Sécurité Sociale des Travailleurs Migrants)

This is an autonomous organization under the supervision of the Ministries for Social Security, Agriculture and Finance. It was founded in 1959 and has three essential missions: a) financial, b) legal and informative, and c) linguistic.

The Centre reimburses health care expenses to:

a) workers insured by a French Social Security Organization and who temporarily stay in another EC country or a country which has a bilateral agreement with France;

b) foreign workers whose families live in their country of origin;

c) old age or invalidity benefit recipients, as well as people who have had an accident at work.

These categories have a right to health care at the expense of the French Social Security Organization which covers them. The Centre reimburses fixed sums on invoices.

Box 8.3: Initiatives to meet the health needs of black and ethnic minorities in the United Kingdom

a) In 1988 the National Association of Health Authorities (NAHA), supported by the Department of Health, produced a report 'Action Not Words' which set out a strategy for health authorities to ensure that they provide a service appropriate to the needs of black and ethnic minorities.

b) The annual report of the Chief Medical Officer in 1991 selected as its main emphasis the health status of people from black and ethnic minorities.

c) There is an advisor on Ethnic Minority health issues at the Department of Health.

d) The 'Health of the Nation' refers to variations in health on ethnic lines but there are no ethnic-specific targets, unlike in the US.

e) Some health authorities have developed strategies to try and improve the health of ethnic minorities. In particular, some which contain large numbers of ethnic minorities are using the contracting mechanism to try and improve access to health care for these groups (e.g. negotiating with providers to supply translating services etc.). In addition, some district health promotion departments have developed materials and programmes for use with different ethnic communities.

f) In its strategy for 1993-8, the Health Education Authority (HEA) stresses that 'the needs of some groups in the population warrant particular attention as the Key Areas (in the "Health of the Nation") are tackled, including the needs of black and ethnic minority groups. The HEA reaffirms its commitment to help make health education accessible and appropriate to black and ethnic minority groups across all Key Areas and other priority areas. In particular, the HEA aims to: provide support for purchasers to identify and meet the health education needs of black and ethnic minority groups: develop partnerships with key organizations and others concerned with the health of black and ethnic minority groups: and disseminate ideas and resources which promote effective and innovative practice in health education with black and ethnic minority groups'.

9

Proposals for the Future Role of the European Community

This chapter summarizes the results of the analysis carried out in previous chapters on the health policy choices available to Member States to improve health and to secure greater efficiency in the use of health resources, and provides recommendations as to the possible role of the Community Institutions to facilitate these processes.

The legal framework within which the European Union may take action in the field of health has evolved considerably since the founding of the Community. The 1956 Treaty of Rome did not mention health specifically although Article 118 enabled the Commission to promote close cooperation in the social field and particularly in matters relating to social security, prevention of occupational accidents and diseases, and occupational hygiene. The Euratom and European Coal and Steel Treaties also contained provision for co-operation in the field of occupational health in respect of the industries concerned.

The 1986 Single European Act amended these earlier treaties and, in Article 100A(3), required the Commission to take, as a base, a high level of protection in its proposals concerning health, safety and environmental and consumer protection, as they relate to the working of the single European market.

The most significant provision in the field of health was introduced in the 1991 European Treaty on European Union. The treaty gives the Union a new competence in public health (Article 129) (Box 9.1), which identifies three areas for Community action: disease prevention and research; health information and education; and the incorporation of health protection requirements in the Community's other policies. However, harmonization of the laws and regulations of Member States are specifically excluded.

Box 9.1: Article 129 of the Treaty on European Union

1. The Community shall contribute towards ensuring a high level of human health protection by encouraging cooperation between the Member States and, if necessary, lending support to their action.

   Community action shall be directed towards the prevention of diseases, in particular the major health scourges, including drug dependence, by promoting research into their causes and their transmission, as well as health information and education.

   Health protection requirements shall form a constituent part of the Community's other policies.

2. Member States shall, in liaison with the Commission, coordinate among themselves their policies and programmes in the areas referred to in paragraph 1. The Commission may, in close contact with the Member States, take any useful initiative to promote such coordination.

3. The Community and the Member States shall foster cooperation with third countries and the competent international organizations in the sphere of public health.

4. In order to contribute to the achievement of the objectives referred to in this Article, the Council:

   • acting in accordance with the procedure referred to in Article 189b, after consulting the Economic and Social Committee and the Committee of the Regions, shall adopt incentive measures, excluding any harmonization of the laws and regulations of the Member States;

   • acting by a qualified majority on a proposal from the Commission, shall adopt recommendations.

Table 9.1 provides an account of a number of health related projects of the European Commission and the responsible Directorates-General.[134] These include DG III (Industry), with responsibility for pharmaceuticals; DG V (Social Affairs), with responsibility for public health and health and safety; and DG XII (Science, Research and Development), with responsibility for biomedical research.

Under the principle of subsidiarity, health services are the responsibility of each Member State. There are, however, certain functions which are more appropriately performed at the level of the Community. The criteria used here to define such functions are:

• where there is a clear need for the coordination of activity or to learn from the experiences of other Member States;

• where functions can be performed cheaper for the Community as a whole;

• where there are issues which cross country boundaries such as epidemics, environmental issues and the consequences of the free movement of personnel;

• where action is needed to standardize definitions so as to make the exchange of information reliable;

• where the actions and policies of the Community have important health implications.

Table 9.1: Overview of the health-related projects of the EC and the responsible Directorates-General (as of December 1993)

Projects	I	III	IV	V	TFE	VI	VIII	XI	XII	XIII	XV	XVI	CP
Medical													
Ageing population				X					X	X			
Disabled		X		X	X		X		X	X	X	X	X
Pharmaceuticals	X	X	X	X			X		X	X	X		X
Biotechnology		X			X	X		X	X	X			
Nutrition/diet	X	X		X		X	X	X	X		X		X
Genetics		X							X				
Immunology				X					X				
AIDS	X			X			X		X			X	
Cancer		X		X		X	X		X	X			
Neuro-sciences									X	X			
Radiation protection				X				X	X	X			
Transplants		X		X					X	X			
Health and safety				X					X				
Tobacco				X		X			X				
Technical Infrastructure													
Medical informatics		X		X			X		X	X			
Biomedical technology		X		X	X		X		X	X	X	X	X
Education/public health													
Education/degrees				X	X		X		X	X	X	X	
Epidemiology				X		X	X	X	X	X		X	X
Health economics/ systems research				X			X		X	X		X	
Social sciences				X			X		X	X		X	
Health promotion				X					X				
Drugs	X			X					X				

Note: Areas of responsibility of Directorate-General (DG): DG I: external relations, DG III: industrial affairs, DG IV: competition, DG V: social affairs, TFE: task force human resources and education, DG VI: agriculture, DG VIII: development, DG XI: environment, DG XII: research and development, DG XIII: telecommunications and information, DG XV: internal market, DG XVI: regional policy, CP: Consumer Policy Unit.

Source: Davaki and Mossialos, (1994) and authors' estimates.

Cost containment policies and health care reforms

Experience to date has shown that the establishment of overall budgets for health care, or for each of its main parts, are the most effective means of containing costs, if they are rigorously enforced, and in some cases backed up by manpower controls. Ways of achieving this have been found, whatever the method of organizing or paying for health care. In particular, it has led to pressure on the hospital sector to reduce lengths of stay, transfer hospitals to other uses or sell them. It has also led to the development of cheaper alternatives to care in hospital. This can be re-enforced by interventions to rationalize hospital stock and the adoption of effective ways of limiting the proliferation of expensive medical equipment.

In some Member States, costs could be saved by increasing the number of general practitioners at the expense of specialists and establishing a pattern of referral, as specialists are more likely to use expensive specialized services when it is not strictly necessary. Moreover, it is increasingly accepted that an excess of doctors in health insurance practice leads to an excess of costs.

Some Member States have found economies by encouraging generic prescribing and imposing positive lists of drugs on their health insurance systems. But the cost of prescriptions depends also on the prices paid for drugs. Prices can be controlled directly or indirectly by controlling profits. At first the reference price systems seemed promising, but there are now doubts about its overall effects. But these measures are in conflict with the long term aim of a Single Market for drugs.

A more fundamental approach is to change the incentives operating on providers to combat supplier-induced demand. One approach is to rationalize fee-for-service payment systems of doctors. Another is to change them to include a substantial element of capitation payment. A third is to pay hospitals on the basis of the type of case treated. It is too early to establish the effects of establishing competitive internal markets. But if these are shown to have more beneficial effects than disadvantages, there is considerable scope for extending this approach throughout the Union by, for example, giving each insured person a free choice of insurer with the contribution income distributed between insurers on the basis of risk, if suitable means of assessing this can be developed. Or where there are not multiple insurers, health authorities or groups of primary care doctors could place contracts for the provision of services.

Cost-sharing can transfer costs from the public sector to the private sector and restrain some costs in total, providing this is not counteracted by extensive private insurance of these co-payments. If such insurance were forbidden or discouraged by the removal of any tax concessions, cost-sharing measures would be more uniformly effective in achieving their objectives. But if they were substantial, or if attempts to restrict the effects on the poor are not very effective, de-insuring in this way can have damaging effects on equity and increase inequalities in access to health care. But a more fundamental question is what can and should be left for individuals to pay themselves.

How far all these types of measure will be sufficient in the long run is an open question. A more fundamental approach is to ensure that all health care provided is effective in improving health outcome. To move towards this objective will be a long process, involving the review and collation of existing knowledge, the acquisition of new knowledge, the continuous assessment of new technologies as they are developed and the development and application of medical practice guidelines.

The Community has established free movement of doctors but this creates problems for Member States who are trying to limit the number of practising doctors. The Community should follow its free movement directive by coordinating the output of doctors in each Member State to the quantity required by need, taking into account the special position of Luxembourg.

Although there is considerable convergence in the policies of cost containment being used in different Member States, much too little is known about the effects of different policies in the longer term. The difficulty is that a measure taken in one Member State is often quickly followed by another in the same Member State, before there is time to see the long term effects of the first measure. This is an area where the Commission could play a useful role in monitoring developments, assessing the success of different policies and communicating the findings to other Member States. Of particular importance is the effects of the major reforms which are aimed to increase the efficiency with which resources are used and which have been recently introduced or planned.

Recommendations

1. The Community should coordinate the output of doctors in Member States to those needed to meet national needs, taking into account the special position of Luxembourg.
2. The Commission should establish a monitoring capacity:
   - to monitor developments in cost containment policies;
   - to assess the success of different policies;
   - to communicate the findings to Member States.

   Of particular importance is to study the effects of the major reforms which have been recently introduced or planned in increasing the efficiency with which resources are used.

Outcomes management and technology assessment

The majority of health care interventions are unevaluated or inadequately evaluated. Information on effectiveness is needed to inform purchasing and planning decisions that will optimize the health benefit for a given level of expenditure. The Community should promote research to define effective health care and ascertain how best to give patients an informed choice. This raises much wider questions than the use of equipment and devices.

There is also a need to disseminate the information that is available. The Community should assist Member States to reduce unnecessary services by the development of medical purchasing guidelines. Some could be established by a systematic review of existing medical literature to learn what treatments – and what steps within those treatments – are necessary and efficient judged by the outcome. This process should build on existing structures such as the Cochrane collaboration. But many new studies will be needed comparing the outcome of different treatment regimes.

There is a scarcity, within Europe, of individuals with the skills required to undertake high quality health service research. The Community should support the development of appropriate educational programmes, drawing on skills in all Member States.

The existing arrangements for technology assessment are likely to lead to gaps and duplication of effort. The Community should co-ordinate technology assessment throughout the Union to establish:

- the effectiveness of both new and existing technology in improving outcome;
- the appropriate uses of these technologies.

Effort should be concentrated in carefully chosen centres so as to achieve economies of scale and develop training centres. Mechanisms should be established for the exchange of information on planned work to avoid duplication of effort.

Recommendations

3. The Community should promote research to define effective health care and ascertain how best to give patients an informed choice.
4. The Community should assist Member States to reduce unnecessary services by the development of medical purchasing guidelines.
5. The Community should support the development of appropriate educational programmes in health services research.
6. The Community should co-ordinate technology assessment throughout the Union.

Priority setting

Both the Community and Member States need to concern itself with health policy in its widest sense and not just with health care. Priorities for health policy should be determined on four criteria:

- the extent and seriousness of the problem;
- whether effective preventive or curative methods are available;
- whether such methods can be used appropriately and efficiently;

- whether it can be left to individual responsibility.

One way of assessing effectiveness is by the health benefits achieved in terms of lower premature mortality, greater ability to function in society and a reduction of the need for care. The use of the quantity of healthy life years is more controversial. Appropriate use includes ethical considerations. Efficiency is concerned with the relationship between the benefits and the cost. It was shown earlier that it is not possible to claim that prevention necessarily lowers curative costs. This is not its central purpose. Nevertheless, the prospective benefits need to be weighed against the costs in the selection of priorities for action.

Health services by themselves can do little to bring about an improvement in the health status of populations, other than in a few areas such as immunization. As shown above, the major causes of ill health lie in the two interrelated sets of factors. The first are environmental, such as housing, traffic, employment and not least the distribution of income. The second are lifestyles, such as smoking, diet, drug abuse and alcohol consumption. This does not mean that health services do not have an essential role in improving the quality of life and can produce valuable improvements in other aspects of health status. But much wider action is needed to secure fundamental improvements of health status and particularly that of the less privileged section of the population.

There are established methods for describing differences in health according to age, sex, social class and geographical area. These are useful but their use is limited when the underlying causes and the potential effects of different actions are unknown and the appropriateness of any action remains doubtful.

An approach which could be taken further is to explain the variations between Member States in the incidence of avoidable deaths. How far are they because patients do not present themselves for treatment and how far is it due to failings in the treatment provided? There is a need for more local studies in different Member States directed at particular conditions.

Following the Alma Ata declaration of 1978, the World Health Organization developed a series of targets known as the 'Health for All' targets. These set out in general terms a series of objectives and means of achieving them, designed to be used by Eastern as well as Western Europe. The task for the future is to sharpen them into more specific objectives for the Union to provide clear guidance for the investment of resources in health and health services, based on priorities for a variety of conditions and services, so as to maximize the improvement obtained in the health status of the population.

A strategic approach to health care planning requires the identification of goals for improvements in the population's health which are as specific as possible. In order to describe accurately the current position and to chart progress towards such goals, it is often necessary to identify intermediate objectives, not only for health, but also for the important determinants of health and the processes which lead to changes in those factors. This may be because the improvement in health status itself is delayed or because health outcomes bear a complicated relationship to multiple causes or factors. Interventions are, therefore, better aimed at individual determinants rather than at specific outcomes. For each area, objectives need to be subdivided into improved health status, risk factor reduction, improved services and protection and the surveillance and data needs.

Priorities for action in the EU

By identifying the common elements in the priorities of Member States (Annex A), where there are potentialities for effective intervention, certain common themes emerge. On this basis, the following 16 areas seem to reflect the views of Member States about what should be priorities for action within the Union:

Smoking
Alcohol-related harm
Drug and substance abuse
Nutrition
Exercise

Mental health
The physical and social environment
Accidents and injuries
Occupational safety and health

Family planning
Maternal and infant health
Blood pressure control
Screening for cancer
Dental health
Physical and sensory disability

Surveillance and control of infectious diseases including sexually transmitted diseases, HIV infection and immunization.

Some of these topics are discussed under the potential for action on disease prevention and health promotion. To develop an operational policy, broad objectives should be accompanied by measurable indicators describing levels of health, the appropriate determinants of health and the levels of relevant service provision. These indicators need also to be sensitive to changes of the size which are anticipated. Once indicators have been identified, targets can be set that will suggest the pace at which progress towards those objectives could reasonably be expected. Targets can be used to highlight important areas of strategy and they are of help in the process of converting policy into programmes. They also provide a tangible means of monitoring progress and can act as a stimulus for the collection of good quality data.

However, there are three potential disadvantages of numerical targets. First, they can lead to spurious priority for that which is measurable. Second, if taken in isolation, they can represent an over simplistic description of policy. Third, unless the target levels are carefully chosen, they can appear either unrealistic and thus be dismissed as unattainable or simply a continuation of existing trends, requiring no additional action to achieve them.

Indicators and targets should be:

- credible, addressing important public health issues which are likely to last;
- clear, easily appraised and understood by a wide audience;
- selective, highlighting areas which are a high priority for action;
- compatible with current public health strategy;
- achievable in the sense that intervention is available or potentially so;
- based on evidence of effectiveness and allowing for delay between intervention and effect;
- balanced, monitoring process through a mixture of process and outcome measures;
- quantifiable, either data is available or there can be proxy indicators for specific recommendations and data collection;
- ethical, respecting the autonomy of individuals and avoiding unnecessary value judgements.

An example of indicators and targets has been developed for the United Kingdom by the Faculty of Public Health Medicine.[135] No complicated modelling technique was used to arrive at the targets. In most cases, the assumptions that would need to be made to construct such a model would give apparent precision which would be falsely reassuring. Trends have been interpreted in the light of what is known of likely future changes in the determinants of health and any expected interventions. An informed assessment of the current evidence relating to the potential impact of preventive interventions on national or international levels of health is a necessary part of target setting.

The task for the future is to develop a set of indicators appropriate for the Union as a whole, taking account of the data which is available or can be made available or developed. Data would need to be gathered for Europe as a whole, in order to provide comparable data for other countries.

Recommendations

Health is the ability to participate in society: inability to participate can be a cause of social exclusion. The aim of health policy should, therefore, be not just to extend life but to improve the quality of life.

Four criteria are suggested in determining priorities for health policy:

- is it essential from a community point of view?
- can action be taken which has been demonstrated to be effective?
- has the use of resources in the choice of method of action been proved to be appropriate and efficient?
- can it not be left to individual responsibility?

7. Member States are urged to consider focusing action on the following 16 priority areas:

Smoking
Alcohol-related harm
Drug and substance abuse
Nutrition
Exercise

Mental health
The physical and social environment
Accidents and injuries
Occupational safety and health

Family planning
Maternal and infant health
Blood pressure control
Screening for cancer
Dental health
Physical and sensory disability

Surveillance and control of infectious diseases including sexually transmitted diseases, HIV infection and immunization.

Action on lifestyles should not be confined to health education. Of more immediate effect are pricing policies and controls on advertising. In the case of the environment, legal regulations and their enforcement with the strong support of economic incentives are among the important ways ahead. But both depend on the development of strong public support.

8. The Community should:

- continue to collect and refine information on avoidable mortality;
- promote local studies in different Member States directed at particular avoidable conditions.

Preventive interventions and health promotion

As shown in Chapter 1, each Member State is faced with a unique pattern of challenges to the health of its population. However, this diversity is a result, at least in part, of differences in the complex interplay of government policies and consumer preferences as they affect factors such as tobacco, alcohol, diet, and transport. Consequently, there is enormous scope for Member States to learn from the experience of others as they develop their own policies. There are also many areas in the field of health promotion and disease prevention where European Union policies have an important role, ranging from agricultural policy through tax harmonization to safety legislation. Some of these problems are described in a volume already published by the Commission.[136]

The effect of increased mobility

Increased mobility has an impact on health through several mechanisms. Mobility of people and goods has always provided an opportunity for the spread of infectious disease. Between 1347 and 1350 the Black Death spread along European trade routes from the Crimea, through Constantinople and Venice, along the Rhone valley, and into Northern Europe, causing death rates of up to 50 per cent in some areas. While the hazards from existing pathogens are less today, the volume of travel is much greater. Surveillance of communicable disease is much better developed in some Member States than in others, with some recent outbreaks of food borne infection in one country only being detected by surveillance of returning holidaymakers in another country. There is a need to support existing efforts to put in place effective surveillance mechanisms that can detect rapidly outbreaks of communicable disease and disseminate information across frontiers. This will include the development of common definitions of infectious diseases, the upgrading, in some Member States, of surveillance networks, and the creation of means of rapid electronic communication.

The risk of spread of communicable disease is accentuated where one Member State has virtually eliminated a disease through immunization but another has not. There is a need to co-ordinate activities at a European level to eliminate those diseases for which this is technically possible, including rubella, pertussis, measles and mumps. This will include disseminating information on the procedures adopted by those Member States that have achieved the highest levels of immunization. An analogous situation is the European Union supported programme to eliminate rabies from the population of foxes and other wild animals.

Increased mobility of workers leads to a situation where individuals from populations with a high prevalence of certain, often inherited, diseases, find themselves in regions where there is little experience of these conditions. An example is thalassaemia. There is a need to promote greater awareness of these conditions among health care professionals who may have had little experience of dealing with them.

Diet

As noted in Chapter 1, there is growing evidence that diet accounts for some of the large differences between Member States in the rates of ischaemic heart disease and some cancers. Diet is a result of a complex interplay between historical patterns of agriculture and availability of other foods, advertising, and personal preference. While no-one can or should be forced to adopt a healthy diet, there is much that can be done to encourage healthy choices. The first step is to recognize that many people living in those Member States where poverty is increasing, most notably the United Kingdom, have no possibility of making any choices without a greater commitment to social justice. The other Member States have signified their commitment to tackle this issue through their signature of the Social Chapter of the Maastricht Treaty. Second, there is a need to improve food labelling and incorporate evidence on how to make labelling more comprehensible, especially to those in lower socio-economic groups. This must reflect growing evidence of the effects of different foodstuffs and, in particular, the effect of substances such as salt, different types of lipid, fish oils, and antioxidants. Third, the price of food is influenced considerably by the complex pattern of agricultural subsidies arising from the Common Agricultural Policy. There is a need to ensure that these subsidies take account of the need to enable people to make healthy dietary choices. Finally, information available to the public is often relatively inaccessible, over-complicated, and, at times, contradictory. There is much that can be done, both nationally and at the European level, to improve this situation and to promote the consumption of foods such as fresh fruit and vegetables.

Alcohol

Several Member States are likely to face major alcohol-related problems in recent years because of tax harmonization and the relaxation on imports. This is already being seen in the south of England as a result of massive importation of relatively cheap beer from France. The impact of cost on alcohol consumption is considerable, with a 1 per cent increase in tax on beer in the United Kingdom associated with a 0.3-0.4 per cent fall in consumption.[137] However this effect is much greater (up to 2.3 per cent) among males aged 18 to 21 who are at greatest risk of alcohol-related traffic death. The health consequences of tax harmonization need to be recognized.

The large effect of national culture on drinking patterns precludes the development of many possible policies at a European level other than those related to pricing. However, changes in alcohol outlets, both in terms of absolute numbers and duration of opening, have been shown to correlate with deaths from motor vehicle accidents.[138]

Tobacco

There is considerable scope, at European level, to tackle tobacco consumption, a substance responsible for the deaths of many thousands of Europeans each year. These include fiscal and legislative measures.

The European Union continues to provide subsidies for tobacco production. These subsidies are primarily a means of redistributing income to rural populations in some parts of the Union and it is argued that much of the tobacco is of low quality and is exported to developing countries. Nonetheless, the imbalance between the very large sums involved in subsidies and the relatively small budget for programmes such as Europe against Cancer have led many to question the commitment of the European Union to promotion of health. There is a strong argument, at least in terms of consistency, for terminating these subsidies and encouraging crop substitution. These funds could then be redeployed to promote health-related activities (see later).

As with alcohol, harmonization of taxes presents a challenge to policies to reduce smoking, especially in those countries where fiscal measures are employed. A price increase of 10 per cent has been shown in the United Kingdom to be associated with a decrease in tobacco consumption of 5-6 per cent.[139]

As noted in Chapter 7, there is now strong evidence that a ban on tobacco advertising would reduce consumption but this is opposed by some Member States. A complication is that some Member States have large export earnings from tobacco. Banning tobacco advertising is also argued against because of the effect in reducing sports sponsorship although states such as Victoria, in Australia, have overcome this by imposing a sponsorship levy on tobacco sales.

In many industrialized countries, both within and without the European Union, the number of places where smoking is permitted is diminishing. This is largely because of the considerable danger from passive smoking. While such policies are largely an issue for individual Member States, the European Union should consider whether it has a role to play in promoting a ban on smoking where there is a supranational dimension, such as on flights within the Union. As many airlines now ban smoking anyway, such a measure is unlikely to be particularly contentious.

Accident prevention
Policies aimed at reducing accidents involve bringing about changes in the environment and in behaviour. An example of the former is introducing legislation to ensure that seat belts are fitted, the latter involves ensuring that they are worn. In many Member States, the emphasis has been on the former rather than the latter. It is recognized in all Member States that wearing seat belts in cars and crash helmets on motor cycles are associated with substantial reductions in death rates. It is up to Member States to ensure that existing legislation is enforced.

The European Union has an important role to play in ensuring that vehicle safety specifications are as high as possible. Attempts to do so have been opposed by the vehicle industry on grounds of cost and competitiveness. It is important that this pressure is resisted.

HIV and AIDS
The great diversity between Member States in the growth of HIV and AIDS reflects

many factors including patterns of migration. Nonetheless, at least some of the difference is likely to be due to variation in the effectiveness of prevention policies. There is considerable scope to learn from experience elsewhere.

Preventive health services
While many of the determinants of health lie outside the formal health care setting, there are also many areas in which early and appropriate interventions can reduce or prevent subsequent development of disease. These include screening and treatment of certain conditions before they cause complications.

Screening
Although there is widespread enthusiasm for screening among the medical profession in many countries, this is less often matched by those responsible for funding and providing health care. To try to set this in context, it is important to review the circumstances when it is appropriate to introduce a screening programme. These are that the disease is important, in terms of its prevalence and consequences, it is possible to detect the disease at a time when effective treatment can reduce mortality or morbidity to a greater extent than would later treatment, and the benefits of early diagnosis and treatment outweigh any disadvantages.

In any given population, the argument about whether to introduce screening is thus dependent on the prevalence of the disease in that population as well as evidence on the effectiveness of screening in other situations. There is good evidence that screening for breast and cervical cancer is effective. Early diagnosis and treatment of mild, moderate or severe hypertension is also effective.[140] This is true not only of pharmacological management of hypertension but also of non-pharmacological management, such as dietary modification. The evidence in favour of screening the general population for elevated plasma lipids is much less obvious, especially when lipid-lowering drugs are used. Although several studies have shown a reduction in cardiovascular deaths, they have either been associated with an increase in deaths from other causes and thus no overall reduction in mortality or a similar reduction in mortality in both intervention and placebo arms of the trial.[141,142,143] Given the high cost of these drugs, there is no evidence to support a population-based screening programme in which they would be used.

The balance of costs and benefits of screening will be different for different diseases in different Member States. Consequently, each Member State must decide for itself what diseases to screen for although the basic principles of whether a screening programme is appropriate should be borne in mind.

Once the decision is made, there is much that can be learnt from the experience of those Member States which already have such programmes. A key issue that arises is that, to be effective, screening programmes must be systematic and cover the entire target population. This requires the development of population registers and integrated diagnostic and curative services. This is easier to achieve in some health systems than in others.

The Commission can play an important role here in co-ordinating policies and programmes.

Recommendations

9. The Community should support existing efforts to put in place effective surveillance mechanisms that can detect rapidly outbreaks of communicable disease and disseminate information across frontiers.

10. The Community should facilitate co-ordination activities at a European level to eliminate, through immunization, those diseases for which this is technically possible.

11. The Community should promote greater awareness of rare diseases affecting migrants among health care professionals who may be called upon to treat them but have little experience of them.

12. The Community should support efforts to enable people to make healthy choices about their diet through:
    * strategies aimed at relieving poverty;
    * improved food labelling;
    * ensuring that agricultural policies are consistent with health;
    * improving understanding of the effect of nutrition on health.

13. The Community should ensure that moves to harmonize taxation do not lead to increases in alcohol or tobacco consumption.

14. The Community should cease subsidies to tobacco growers and encourage crop substitution.

15. The Community should introduce a ban on tobacco advertising.

16. The Community should explore ways in which it might act to increase the number of smoke free locations.

17. The Community should ensure that safety legislation emphasizes safety and is not diluted by unjustified arguments about competitiveness.

18. The Community should facilitate the process of learning from experience of health promotion and disease prevention in different Member States.

Inequalities in health and the use of health services

As noted earlier in this paper, there are substantial differences in health status between Member States, and within them between social classes, occupational groups, regions, the sexes and ethnic groups. The causes of these differences are not fully understood. There are also substantial differences in the provision of services and in the use of health services, though these differences do not appear to be factors influencing aggregate health status: those with greater health needs need to use more health services and these are disproportionately among the lower socioeconomic groups.

This raises a whole series of questions. What are (and what should be) the objectives of policy towards inequities in health and health care? Can these be formulated in a fashion that is both generally acceptable and sufficiently specific to be useful? What is the most useful way of defining and measuring health from the point of view of health inequities? Once that is decided, which inequality measure should be used, and what do the different measures tell us? To what extent are observed health inequities the outcome of social selection? What other factors might explain their persistence? What are the main factors that lead to unjustifiable inequality in the utilization of health services? What are the principal socioeconomic factors that affect health? In what way do they affect health; how does their influence operate? How much of an influence on health is medical care? What is its importance relative to that of socioeconomic factors? How effective have different Member States been in reducing inequities in health and health care? How far can differences in effectiveness be explained by differences in institutions? What are the principal political impediments to the implementation of effective inequality-reducing policies?

This is a large area for policy-relevant research with great opportunities for useful comparisons to be made between the experiences of different Member States. Widening inequalities between racial, gender or socioeconomic groups are unacceptable and there needs to be a concerted effort to apply existing knowledge, while new knowledge is acquired.

Meanwhile the Community should press ahead with its initiative to establish a minimum income for each Member State as evidence is accumulating that inadequate income itself is health-damaging.

Recommendations

19. The Community should pool the experience of different Member States to acquire a better knowledge of the causes of health inequalities and develop remedial policies.
20. The Community should press ahead with its initiative to establish a minimum income in each Member State for health as well as other reasons.
21. Member States are urged to make a concerted effort to identify the causes and develop relevant policies with the aim of reducing inequalities in health and avoidable deaths within and between Member States.

Services for migrants and ethnic minorities

Migrant populations have specific health needs for several reasons which were analysed earlier. It is necessary to ensure that preventive and curative services are designed explicitly to meet their needs.

Member States vary significantly in the extent to which they have made specific provision for the needs of migrants and ethnic minorities. There are also differences in the way in which migrants and ethnic minorities are viewed in different countries.

Their needs are often not regarded as a priority. The research available indicates that it is insufficient to assume that by simply making specific services available, they will be used.

Recommendation

22. The Community should sponsor the exchange of information on approaches to meeting the health needs of migrants, taking into account the diversity of patterns of migration into and within the Union.

Learning from different experiences

One of the tasks of the Community in coordinating health policy is to develop a European Health Services Information facility. Its first assignment would be to develop, in collaboration with WHO and the OECD, common standards and definitions so that comparative studies can be undertaken to assess possible variations in health needs, utilization, health expenditure and outcome. It should develop a Union-wide system of surveillance of the incidence of both communicable and other diseases in order to identify new problems as they arise and identify the causes of changes in incidence. It should develop co-operative arrangements for the evaluation of methods of treatment, particularly those using high technology, capitalizing on the variations in methods of treatment in the different Member States. It should investigate the aetiology of some of the major causes of mortality and morbidity in order to identify possible preventive strategies. These studies should be concerned with such conditions as arthritis, neurological disorders and psychiatric conditions where little research has been undertaken. It should sponsor appropriate experiments to evaluate different approaches to the control of diseases for which preventive measures are known, such as cancer of the lung and smoking and determine the cost-effectiveness of the different approaches. It should build on the successful experience of the 'Europe against Cancer' programme.

It should develop methods for identifying the health consequences of migration and ways of abating the harmful effects. It should take the opportunity presented by migration to study some of the possible causes of common diseases which vary in incidence and prevalence between the host and the originating country to provide a better assessment of the contributions of environmental factors in aetiology. It should encourage the exchange of information on approaches to meeting the health needs of migrants, taking account of the diversity of patterns of migration into and within the Union.

One of the functions of the Commission should be to compile a periodic report on the health of the Member States, using the sharper types of indicator proposed earlier. Lessons can be learnt by comparing the incidence and prevalence of various diseases in different environments, taking advantage of the heterogeneity of the populations, services and customs in the Community. This is one possible way to determine their causes and prevent occurrence.

Skills to undertake the tasks of evaluation and assessment of needs are unevenly distributed between Member States. There are as yet no common standards in training for public health. The Community needs to give a strong lead in developing such standards and promoting public health education.

Recommendations

23. The Community should develop a European Health Services Information Facility to:
    - develop a set of indicators appropriate for the Community as a whole, taking account of the data which is available or can be made available or developed. Data would need to be gathered for Europe as a whole, in order to provide comparable data for other countries;
    - in collaboration other international agencies, work out common standards and definitions so that comparative studies can be undertaken to assess possible variations in health needs, utilization, health expenditure and outcome;
    - establish a Union-wide system of surveillance;
    - compare the incidence and prevalence of various diseases in different environments, taking advantage of the heterogeneity of the populations, services and customs in the Union;
    - make use of the existing wide variation in the incidence of many diseases to investigate the aetiology of major causes of mortality and morbidity so as to identify possible preventive strategies;
    - sponsor appropriate experiments in the control of diseases for which preventive measures are known, building on the successful experience of 'Europe against Cancer';
    - identify the health consequences of migration and develop ways of abating the harmful effects.
24. The Commission should compile a periodic report on the health of the people of the Union using the above indicators.
25. The Community should give a lead in the development of common standards for training in public health and promote public health education to make the above easier to accomplish.
26. The Community should find the extra finance for the above by the reduction of subsidies to those agricultural commodities which can be damaging to health.

Conclusion

The focus of this book is on health services. But as made clear earlier, the fundamental causes of ill-health can only be remedied by changes in the inter-related areas of lifestyle and environment. Here lies the key to reducing the incidence of such illnesses as cancer and coronary artery disease or improving sexual or mental health. The Commission has already developed policies in such fields as AIDS, tobacco, alcohol, drug abuse, the environment and health and safety at work: research programmes are already directed at nutrition, cardiovascular diseases, mental illness and the problems associated with ageing. Health services have only a minor part to play in combatting the major scourges that afflict the people of the Union, but the large resources used in providing them can be used more effectively. The Member States can collectively learn how best to achieve this. There is, therefore, a vital coordinating role for the Community to play in the coming years.

Annex A

Official Priorities of Member States

The priorities identified by governments of Member States have been set out in a variety of documents. All have endorsed the WHO 'Health for All' targets and most have produced reports describing the health status of their populations and setting out some of the strategies required to achieve these targets. There is, however, variation in the extent to which these strategies have been implemented. Some Member States have also published documents identifying key areas in health or health care which will receive special attention. Finally, during the development of the Commission framework for action in the field of public health, Member States identified their priorities in the field of prevention. The following paragraphs represent an attempt to distil the key features of these documents.

In **Belgium**, the French Community has the following priorities – AIDS, drug abuse, the elderly, mental illness, immigrants and the disadvantaged. The Flemish Community has developed a comprehensive Health Promotion and Prevention Strategy based on co-ordination of local and regional initiatives, increasing inter-sectoral collaboration, ensuring adequate resources for specific preventive actions, and surveillance of trends in data related to public health.

The **Danish** government published 'The Health Promotion Programme of the Government of Denmark' in 1989. This gave priority to action against cancer, cardiovascular disease, accidents, psychological problems, and musculo-skeletal disease. Arising from this, specific programmes have been established in the areas of nutrition, tobacco and alcohol. Following a change of government in 1993, policy is under review. In the field of health care, the government over the past two decades has established a series of commissions that have made recommendations, among others, for an increased emphasis on primary care.

Spain has established priorities in three categories. For health promotion the emphasis is on tobacco, exercise, alcohol abuse, nutrition. In the environment the emphasis is on biological, physical, chemical and work-related risks. In the health system the emphasis is placed on public health, primary care, maternity and infant care, oral hygiene and rehabilitation. Spain is also carrying forward the 'Health for All' strategy through the 'Healthy Cities' programme which involves over 30 municipal authorities.

In **France**, a 'Haut Comité de la Santé Publique' has been established and has produced a preliminary report on health priorities but this is under review by the government. The report described the main health issues for different population groups and the main health problems (cardiovascular disease, infectious and communicable disease, cancer, mental health, suicides and AIDS). Particular emphasis was given to illicit drugs, tobacco, alcohol, psychotropic medicines and environmental health.

In **Greece**, priorities are cancer, AIDS, cardiovascular disease, blood and blood products supply, blood-related hereditary disease, accidents, drugs, mental health and infectious disease.

The **Irish** government has published a series of key principles in the field of health care, as part of a general review of government policy, the 'Programme for Economic and Social Progress'. These include increased development of primary and community care, and services for elderly, physically and mentally handicapped and mentally ill people. A National Health Strategy for effective health care in the 1990s has recently been published[144] with the aim of ensuring that improving health and quality of life become the unifying focus of health activity. Hard targets are presented for reductions in risk factors associated with premature mortality and in the incidence of cardiovascular disease, cancers and accidents. In addition the improvement in a wide range of health indicators is targeted.

In **Italy**, preventive actions are focused on the environment and health, lifestyle related problems, health protection at work, and the prevention of infectious diseases. Among lifestyle related factors, there is an emphasis on tobacco, drug abuse, AIDS, and nutrition.

The **Luxembourg** government has recently published a document 'Santé pour Tous'. The objectives are the reduction of premature and avoidable deaths and generally improving the health status of the population. It has laid down precise objectives and specific targets.

The **Netherlands** government published a discussion document, 'Health 2000 Memorandum', in 1986. This contained an analysis of the health status of the Dutch population but no recommendations on policy. This led to further discussion documents and, in 1992, 'A strategy for health' was published, although quantified health targets which had been in earlier documents were dropped. The disease prevention programme consists of vaccination, screening of PKU and CHT, cervix and breast cancer and counselling for mothers and young children. The health promotion programme emphasizes alcohol abuse, AIDS, tobacco and mental health for groups at risk. Inter-sectoral action in the field of labour concentrates on disablement, environment, safety and health inequalities. In 1992, a policy document was issued advocating the strengthening of preventive activities undertaken in primary care.

The Ministry of Health, Welfare and Cultural Affairs has invited the National Institute of Public Health and Environmental Protection to produce a document on 'Long range forecasts' which will be used to evaluate existing policy and to steer future developments.

In **Portugal**, a recently published plan for 1994-9 defines the major objectives of health policy:

- to develop health programmes for specific groups: maternal and child health, support to the aged, cancer, drug abuse, AIDS, tobacco and alcohol;
- to construct new health facilities such as hospitals and health centres;
- staff training;
- promotion of quality assurance and optimization of the management of the NHS.

The **United Kingdom** government has set out its priorities in a document 'The Health of the Nation'. This was originally issued as a discussion document (i.e. a Green Paper) which set out for consultation the Government's proposals for the development of a health strategy for England. 'The Health of the Nation', issued in 1992, and the subsequent handbooks outline the Government's priorities for health promotion. The five key areas chosen are: coronary heart disease and stroke; cancers (lung, cervical, breast, skin); mental illness; HIV/AIDS and sexual health; and accidents. In addition, priorities for service delivery have been established in recent years. These include: the development of breast screening services and strengthening of cervical screening services; improvements in maternity services; reduction of waiting lists and expansion of specified acute services; the development of services for elderly people, people with mental health problems and those with physical disabilities, with an emphasis on a move away from institutional care, the strengthening of primary care (especially in inner cities), and the development of quality assurance.

Annex B

Recommendations on the Role of Community Institutions

Cost containment policies and health care reforms
1. The Community should coordinate the output of doctors in Member States to those needed to meet national needs, taking into account the special position of Luxembourg.
2. The Commission should establish a monitoring capacity:
   - to monitor developments in cost containment policies;
   - to assess the success of different policies;
   - to communicate the findings to Member States.

   Of particular importance is to study the effects of the major reforms which have been recently introduced or planned in increasing the efficiency with which resources are used.

Outcomes management and technology assessment
3. The Community should promote research to define effective health care and ascertain how best to give patients an informed choice.
4. The Community should assist Member States to reduce unnecessary services by the development of medical purchasing guidelines.
5. The Community should support the development of appropriate educational programmes in health services research.
6. The Community should co-ordinate technology assessment throughout the Union.

Priority setting
Health is the ability to participate in society: inability to participate can be a cause of social exclusion. The aim of health policy should, therefore, be not just to extend life but to improve the quality of life.

Five criteria are suggested in determining priorities for health policy:

a) is it essential from a community point of view?
b) can action be taken which has been demonstrated to be effective?
c) is rehabilitation possible?
d) has the use of resources in the choice of method of action been proved to be appropriate and efficient?
e) can it be left to individual responsibility?
7. Member States are urged to focus action on the following 16 priority areas:
Smoking
Alcohol-related harm
Drug and substance abuse
Nutrition
Exercise
Mental health
The physical and social environment
Accidents and injuries
Occupational safety and health
Family planning
Maternal and infant health
Blood pressure control
Screening for cancer
Dental health
Physical and sensory disability
Surveillance and control of infectious diseases including sexually transmitted diseases, HIV infection and immunization.
Action on lifestyles should not be confined to health promotion. Of more immediate effect are pricing policies and controls on advertising. In the case of the environment, legal regulations and their enforcement with the strong support of economic incentives are among the important ways ahead. But both depend on the development of strong public support.
8. The Community should:
   • continue to collect and refine information on avoidable mortality;
   • promote local studies in different Member States directed at particular avoidable conditions.

Preventive interventions and health promotion
9. The Community should support existing efforts to put in place effective surveillance mechanisms that can detect rapidly outbreaks of communicable disease and disseminate information across frontiers.
10. The Community should facilitate co-ordination activities at a European level to eliminate, through immunization, those diseases for which this is technically possible.
11. The Community should promote greater awareness of rare diseases affecting migrants among health care professionals who may be called upon to treat them

but have little experience of them.

12. The Community should support efforts to enable people to make healthy choices about their diet through:
    - strategies aimed at relieving poverty;
    - improved food labelling;
    - ensuring that agricultural policies are consistent with health;
    - improving understanding of the effect of nutrition on health.
13. The Community should ensure that moves to harmonize taxation do not lead to increases in alcohol or tobacco consumption.
14. The Community should cease subsidies to tobacco growers and encourage crop substitution.
15. The Community should introduce a ban on tobacco advertising.
16. The Community should explore ways in which it might act to increase the number of smoke free locations.
17. The Community should ensure that safety legislation emphasizes safety and is not diluted by unjustified arguments about competitiveness.
18. The Community should facilitate the process of learning from experience of health promotion and disease prevention in different Member States.

Inequalities in health and the use of health services

19. The Community should pool the experience of different Member States to acquire a better knowledge of the causes of health inequities and develop remedial policies.
20. The Community should press ahead with its initiative to establish a minimum income in each Member State for health as well as other reasons.
21. Member States are urged to make a concerted effort to identify the causes and develop relevant policies with the aim of reducing inequities in health and avoidable deaths within and between Member States.

Services for migrants and ethnic minorities

22. The Community should sponsor the exchange of information on approaches to meeting the health needs of migrants, taking into account the diversity of patterns of migration into and within the Union.

Learning from different experiences

23. The Community should develop a European Health Services Information Facility to:
    - develop a set of indicators appropriate for the Community as a whole, taking account of the data which is available or can be made available or developed. Data would need to be gathered for Europe as a whole, in order to provide comparable data for other countries;
    - in collaboration with other international agencies, work out common standards and definitions so that comparative studies can be undertaken to assess pos-

sible variations in health needs, utilization, health expenditure and outcome;
- establish a union-wide system of surveillance;
- compare the incidence and prevalence of various diseases in different environments, taking advantage of the heterogeneity of the populations, services and customs in the Union;
- make use of the existing wide variation in the incidence of many diseases to investigate the aetiology of major causes of mortality and morbidity so as to identify possible preventive strategies;
- sponsor appropriate experiments in the control of diseases for which preventive measures are known, building on the successful experience of 'Europe against Cancer';
- identify the health consequences of migration and develop ways of abating the harmful effects.

24. The Commission should compile a periodic report on the health of the people of the Union using the above indicators.

25. The Community should give a lead in the development of common standards for training in public health and promote public health education to make the above easier to accomplish.

26. The Community should find the extra finance for the above by the reduction of subsidies to those agricultural commodities which can be damaging to health.

References

1   Evans R.W., 'Health care technology and the inevitability of resource alloca-
    tion and rationing decisions – part II', *Journal of the American Medical Asso-
    ciation*, Vol. 249. 1983, pp. 2208-17.
2   Waldman S., 'Effect of changing technology on hospital costs', *Social Security
    Bulletin*, Vol. 35, 1972, pp. 28-30.
3   Davis K., 'The role of technology, demand and labor markets in the determina-
    tion of hospital costs', Perlman M. (ed.), *The economics of health and medical
    care*, New York, John Wiley & Sons, 1974, pp. 283-301.
4   Commission of the European Communities, Commission communication on
    the framework for action in the field of public health, COM(93) 559, Brussels,
    24 November 1993.
5   The source of data for this section is the WHO data base, covering the period
    1970 to 1991. Except for motor vehicles accidents, death rates are among those
    aged 0 to 64 as it is often difficult to assign a single cause of death to the
    elderly. This age range was chosen to correspond with the WHO data base and
    the upper limit has no other significance.
6   Vartiainen E., Puska P., Pekkanen J., Tuomilehto J., Jousilahti P., 'Changes in
    risk factors explain changes in mortality from ischaemic heart disease in Fin-
    land', *British Medical Journal*, Vol. 309, 1994, pp. 23-7.
7   Sytkowski P.A., Kannel W.B., D'Agostino R.B., 'Changes in risk factors and
    the decline in mortality from cardiovascular disease', *New England Journal of
    Medicine*, Vol. 23, 1990, pp. 1635-41.
8   de Lorgeril M., Renaud S., Mamelle N., Salen P., Martin J-L., Monjaud I.,
    Guidollet J., Touboul P., Delaye J., 'Mediterranean alpha-linoleic acid-rich diet
    in secondary prevention of coronary heart disease', *Lancet*, Vol. 343, 1994, pp.
    1454-9.
9   Burr M.L., Fehily A.M., Gilbert J.F. et al., 'Effects of changes in fat, fish and

153

fibre intakes on death and myocardial infarction: diet and reinfarction trial (DART)', *Lancet*, Vol ii, 1989, pp. 757-61.

[10] Block G., Patterson B., Surbar A., 'Fruit, vegetables, and cancer prevention: a review of the epidemiological evidence', *Nutrition and Cancer*, Vol. 18, 1992, pp. 1-29.

[11] Austoker J., 'Diet and cancer', *British Medical Journal*, Vol. 308, 1994, pp. 1610-4.

[12] European Union, Biomedical and Health Research, Vol. 4, 1993, (insert) pp. 1-16.

[13] Commission of the European Communities, Communication on an action programme on road safety, COM(93) 246, Brussels, 9 June 1993.

[14] MacCoun R., Aaron J.S., Kahan J.P., Reuter P., 'Drug policies and problems: the promise and pitfalls of cross-national comparison' in Heather N., Wodak A., Nadelman E., O'Hare P. (eds.), *Psychoactive drugs and harm reduction: from faith to science*, London, Whurr, 1993, pp. 103-7.

[15] World Health Organisation, *Targets for Health for All*, WHO, Copenhagen, 1985.

[16] Whitehead M., *The Concepts and Principles of Equity and Health*, WHO, Copenhagen, 1990, p. 6.

[17] Whitehead M., *The Health Divide* in Whitehead, M., (ed.) *Inequalities in Health*, Penguin, London, 1992.

[18] Power C., 'Health and social inequality in Europe', *British Medical Journal*, Vol. 308, 1994, pp. 1153-56.

[19] Le Grand J., 'An international comparison of distributions of ages-at-death', in Fox J., (ed.), *Health Inequalities in European Countries*, Gower, London, 1989.

[20] Whitehead M., op.cit., 1992, pp. 290-310.

[21] Illsley R., and Svensson P., 'Health inequalities in Europe', *Social Science and Medicine*, Vol. 31, 1990, pp. 223-420.

[22] Fox, J., and Leichter H.M., 'The Ups and Downs of Oregon's Rationing Plan', *Health Affairs*, Vol. 12, No. 2, 1993, pp. 66-70.

[23] Illsley R., and Le Grand J., 'Regional inequalities in mortality', *Journal of Epidemiology and Community Health*, Vol. 47, 1993, pp. 444-9.

[24] Illsley R., and Le Grand J., 'The measurement of inequality in health', in Williams A., (ed.) *Economics and Health*, Macmillan, London, 1987, pp. 12-36.

[25] Phillimore P., Beattie A., Townsend P., 'Widening inequality of health in Northern England 1981-91', *British Medical Journal*, Vol. 308, 1994, pp. 1125-8.

[26] Holstein B., 'Denmark country paper' *Inequalities in Health and Health Care*, NHV report 1985:5 quoted in Whitehead M., op. cit., 1992, p. 301.

[27] Kunst A., and Mackenbach J., *An International Comparison of Socio-economic Inequalities in Mortality*, Department of Public Health and Social Medicine, Rotterdam, 1992.

[28] Kunst A., Guerts J., and van den Berg J., *International Variation in Socio-economic*

Inequalities in Self-Reported Health, Netherlands Central Bureau of Statistics and Erasmus University, Rotterdam, 1992.

29 Power C., op. cit.

30 Davey Smith G., Blane D., Bartley M., 'Explanations for socio-economic differentials in mortality: evidence from Britain and elsewhere', *European Journal of Public Health*, Vol. 4, 1994, pp. 131-44.

31 Van Doorslaer E., Wagstaff A., and Rutten F., *Equity in the Finance and Delivery of Health Care*, Commission of the European Communities, Research Series No. 8, Oxford University Press, Oxford, 1992.

32 Black D., *Inequalities in Health*, Report of a research working group chaired by Sir Douglas Black, Department of Health and Social Security, London, 1980.

33 *Ibid.*, p. 170.

34 Power, op. cit, p. 1153.

35 Le Grand J., 'Inequalities in health: some international comparisons', *European Economic Review*, Vol. 31, 1987, pp. 182-91.

36 Wilkinson R.S., 'National mortality rates: the impact of inequality', *American Journal of Public Health*, Vol. 82, 1992, pp. 1082-4.

37 Reading R., Clover A., Openshaw S., and Jarvis S., 'Do interventions that improve immunisation uptake also reduce social inequalities in uptake?', *British Medical Journal*, Vol. 308, No. 6937, 1994, pp. 1142-1444.

38 Seng C., Lessof L., McKee M., 'Who's on the fiddle?', *Health Service Journal*, Vol. 103, 1993, pp. 16-7.

39 Schwefel, D., (ed.), *Indicators and Trends in Health and Health Care*, Springer Verlag, Berlin-Heidelberg, Germany, 1987.

40 OECD, *Health Care Systems in Transition: the search for efficiency*, OECD, Paris, 1990.

41 In Denmark, health visiting, home nursing and nursing homes are classified as social services.

42 The ratio of practising doctors given by the OECD for Italy is 1.3 per 1000 population and includes only public hospital-based physicians. Thus, the ratio for Italy has been obtained from another source and refers to the total number of registered doctors as shown in Federazione Nazionale degli Ordini dei Medici, *Ufficio Statistico*, Roma 1990. This source, however, may slightly overstate the number of practising doctors as it includes those who are unemployed and those who work in other sectors such as in the pharmaceutical industry.

43 Roemer M., *National Health Systems of the World*, Vol. I, Oxford University Press, New York, 1991.

44 A detailed account of cost containment measures in each Member State is published separately as Abel-Smith, B. and Mossialos, E., 'Cost containment and Health Care Reform: a Study of the European Union', *Health Policy*, 28(2), 1994, pp.89-132.

45 Sheldon T., 'Chronic sick penalised in the Netherlands', *British Medical Journal*, Vol. 308, 1994, p. 1059.

46 Evans R.W., 'Health care technology and the inevitability of resource allocation and rationing decisions – part I', *Journal of the American Medical Association*, Vol. 249, No. 15, 1983, pp. 2047-53.

47 Coulter A., and Bradlow J., 'Effect of NHS reforms on general practitioners' referral patterns', *British Medical Journal*, Vol. 306, 1993, p. 433-7.

48 Sheldon T., 'Dutch health reforms have failed, say Ministers', *British Medical Journal*, Vol. 308, 1994, p. 936.

49 Dixon J., Dinwoodie M., Hodson D., Dodd S., Poltorak T., Garrett C., Rice P., Doncaster I., Williams M., 'Distribution of NHS funds between fundholding and non-fundholding practices', *British Medical Journal*, Vol. 308, 1994, pp. 30-4.

50 Clarke A., McKee M., 'The consultant episode: an unhelpful measure', *British Medical Journal*, Vol. 305, 1992, pp. 1307-8.

51 Wennberg J.E., Freeman J.L., Culp W.J., 'Are hospital services rationed in New Haven or over-utilised in Boston?', *Lancet*, Vol. i, 1987, pp. 1185-9.

52 Wennberg J.E., 'Innovation and the Policies of Limits in a Changing Health Care Economy', in: Gelijns A.C. (ed.), *Technology and Health Care in an Era of Limits*, National Academy Press, Washington D.C., 1992, pp. 16-7.

53 *ibid.*, p. 18-29.

54 Chappel N.L., 'The future of health care in Canada', *Journal of Social Policy*, Vol. 22, Part. 4, 1993, p. 495.

55 Veatch R.M., 'The Oregon Experiment: Needless and Real Worries' in Strosberg M.A. et al., *Rationing America's Medical Care: the Oregon Plan and Beyond*, The Brookings Institution, Washington D.C., 1992, p. 88.

56 Grimshaw J., Russell I.T., 'Effect of clinical guidelines on medical practice: a systematic review of rigorous evaluations', *Lancet*, Vol. 342, 1993, pp. 1317-22.

57 US General Accounting Office, *Medical Malpractice: Maine's use of practice guidelines to reduce costs*, US Government Printing Office, GAO/HRD-94-8, 1994.

58 Lomas J. et al., 'A taxonomy and critical review of tested strategies for the application of clinical practice recommendations: from official to individual clinical policy', *American Journal of Preventive Medicine*, Vol. 4 (Supplement), 1988, pp. 77-84.

59 Grimshaw J.M., Russell I.T., 'Achieving health gain through clinical guidelines: I. Developing scientifically valid guidelines', *Quality in Health Care*, Vol. 2, 1993, pp. 243-8.

60 McKee M., Sanderson C., 'An approach to assessing need for elective surgery: the importance of thresholds', *Proceedings of the Conference of the European Healthcare Management Association*, ENS/EHMA, Madrid, 1992.

61 Wilcock G.K., 'The prevalence of osteoarthrosis of the hip requiring total hip replacement in the elderly', *International Journal of Epidemiology*, Vol. 8, 1979, pp. 247-50.

62 Wormwald R.P.L., Wright L.A., Courtney P., Beaumont B., Haines A.P., 'Visual problems in the elderly population and implications for services', *British Medical Journal*, Vol. 304, 1992, pp. 1226-9.

63 Hunter D., McKee M., Sanderson C., Black N., 'Appropriate indications for prostatectomy – results of a consensus panel', *Journal of Epidemiology of Community Health*, Vol. 48, 1994, pp. 58-64.

64 For example, a positron emission tomography scanner costs about 8 million ECUs.

65 Fineberg H.V. and Hiatt H.H., 'Evaluation of medical practices: the case for technology assessment', *The New England Journal of Medicine*, Vol. 301, No. 20, 1979, pp. 1086-91.

66 Tugwell P. et al., 'A framework for the evaluation of technology: the technology assessment iterative loop', in Feeny D. et al. (eds.), *Health care technology: effectiveness, efficiency and public policy*, The Institute for Research on Public Policy, Montreal, 1986.

67 Glasser J.H., 'The aims and methods of technology assessment', *Health Policy*, Vol. 9, 1988, pp. 241-50.

68 Fuchs V.R. and Garber A.M., 'The new technology assessment', *The New England Journal of Medicine*, Vol. 323, No. 10, 1990, pp. 673-7.

69 Drummond M.F. et al., *'Methods for the economic evaluation of health care programmes'*, Oxford University Press, Oxford, 1987.

70 Stocking B. (ed.), *Expensive health technology: regulatory and administrative mechanisms in Europe*, Oxford University Press, Oxford, 1988.

71 *First Report to the Central Research and Development Committee from the Standing Group on Health Technology*, NHS Management Executive, Leeds, 1993.

72 The Swedish Council on Technology Assessment in Health Care, *Health Care Technology Assessment programs – a review of selected programs in different countries*, SBU, Stockholm, 1993.

73 Vig N.J., 'Parliamentary technology assessment in Europe: a comparative perspective', in Bryner G.C.(ed.), *Science, technology and politics: policy analysis in Congress*, Westview Press, Boulder, 1992.

74 Drummond M.F. (ed.), *Economic appraisal of health technology in the European Community*, Oxford Medical Publications, Oxford, 1987.

75 France G., 'Centralized versus decentralized research funding: impact on technology evaluation in Italy', *Social Science and Medicine*, Vol. 38, No. 12, 1994, pp. 1635-43.

76 Rutten F., and van der Linden J-W., 'Integration of economic appraisal and health care policy in a health insurance system; the Dutch case', *Social Science and Medicine*, Vol. 38, No. 12, 1994, pp. 1609-15.

77 Granados A. and Borras J.M., 'Technology assessment in Catalonia: integrating economic appraisal', *Social Science and Medicine*, Vol. 38, No. 12, 1994, pp. 1643-7.

78 Henshall C. and Drummond M.F., 'Economic appraisal in the British National

Health service: implications of recent developments', *Social Science and Medicine*, Vol. 38, No. 12, 1994, pp. 1615-25.

79 CDRC Standing Group on Health Technology, *First Report to the Central Research and Development Committee*, Department of Health, Leeds, 1993.

80 McKee M., Clarke A., Kornitzer M., Gheyssens H., Krasnik A., Brand H., Levett J., Bolumar F., Chambaud L., Herity B., Auxilia F., Castaldi S., Landheer T., Lopes Dias J., Briz T., 'Public health medicine training in the European Community: is there scope for harmonisation?', *European Journal of Public Health*, Vol. 2, 1992, pp. 45-53.

81 Mills A., Vaughan J.P., Smith D.L. and Tabibzadeh I., *Health system decentralisation*, WHO, Geneva, 1990.

82 City of Copenhagen, *Healthy City Plan 1994-97*, Copenhagen Health Services, Copenhagen, 1994.

83 IDIS, *Gesundheits-berichterstattung*, IDIS, Bielefeld, 1993.

84 Ministry of Health, Welfare and Cultural Affairs, *Report on Choices in Health Care*, 1993.

85 Ham C., 'Priority setting in the NHS: reports from six districts', *British Medical Journal*, Vol. 307, 1993, pp. 435-8.

86 Heginbotham C., 'Health care priority setting: a survey of doctors, managers and the general public'. British Medical Journal, *Rationing in Action*, BMJ Publishing Group, 1993.

87 Ham C., op. cit.

88 Klein R. and Redmayne S., *Pattern of Priorities: A study of the purchasing and rationing policies of health authorities*, National Association of Health Authorities and Trusts, Birmingham, 1992.

89 Freemantle N., Maynard A., 'Something rotten in the state of clinical and economic evaluations?' *Health Economics*, Vol. 3, 1994, pp. 63-7.

90 Karcher H.L., 'German hospital directors accused of bribery', *British Medical Journal*, Vol. 308, 1994, pp. 1588-9.

91 Klein R., 'Health care reform: the global search for utopia', *British Medical Journal*, Vol. 307, 1993, p. 752.

92 Bjerregaard P. and Jorgensen-Kamper F., *Health Services Research in Denmark*, the Danish Institute for Clinical Epidemiology, Copenhagen, 1992.

93 Spanjer M., 'How to reorganise Dutch medical research', *Lancet*, Vol. 343, February 26, 1994.

94 Holland W., *European Community Atlas of 'avoidable death'*, second edition, Volume 1, Oxford University Press, Oxford, 1991.

95 Stehbens W.E., 'An appraisal of the epidemic rise of coronary heart disease and its decline', *Lancet*, Vol. i, 1987, pp. 606-9.

96 Barker D.J.P. (ed.), *'Fetal and infant origins of adult disease'*, BMJ Publishing Group, London, 1992.

97 World Bank, *Investing in health: World Development Report 1993*, World Bank, Washington, 1993.

[98] See Rosser R.M. and Watts V.C., 'The Measurement of Hospital Output', *International Journal of Epidemiology*, Vol. 1, No. 4, 1972, pp. 361-69 and Rosser R. and Kind P., 'A Scale of Valuation of States of Illness: Is there a consensus', *International Journal of Epidemiology*, Vol. 7, No. 4, 1978, pp. 347-58.

[99] Gudex C., *QALYS and their use by the Health Service*, Discussion paper No. 20, Centre for Health Economics, York University, 1986.

[100] Rosser R. and Kind P., 'A scale of valuations of states of illness' *International Journal of Epidemiology*, Vol. 7, No. 4, 1978, pp. 347-58.

[101] Kaplan R. et al., 'Effects of Number rating Scale Points Upon Utilities in a Quality Well-being scale', *Medical Care*, Vol. 29, No. 10, 1991.

[102] Fox D.M., and Leichter H.M., 'The Ups and Downs of Oregon's Rationing Plan', *Health Affairs*, Vol. 12, No. 2, 1993, pp. 66-70.

[103] Health Care and Medical Priorities Commission, *No Easy Choices: the difficult priorities of health care*, Swedish Government Official Reports, Stockholm, 1993.

[104] Health Security Act, 1993.

[105] Core Services Committee, *The Best of Health 2: How we decide on the health and disability support services we value most*, PO Box 5013, Wellington, New Zealand, 1993.

[106] Advisory Council for the Concerted Action in Health Care, *Health Care and Health Insurance 2000: Individual-responsibility, subsidiarity and solidarity in a changing environment*, Expert Opinion Report, Bonn, 1994 (Abbreviated Version), pp. 5 and 36.

[107] Ministry of Welfare, Health and Cultural Affairs, *op. cit.*, 1992.

[108] Demicheli V. and Jefferson T.O., 'Cost-benefit analysis of the introduction of mass vaccination against Hepatitis B in Italy', *Journal of Public Health Medicine*, 1992, Vol. 14, pp. 367-75.

[109] Showstack J.A., Budetti P.P. and Minkler D., 'Factors associated with birth weight: an exploration of the roles of prenatal care and length of gestation', *American Journal of Public Health*, Vol. 74, 1984, pp. 1003-8.

[110] Quick J.D., Greenlick M.R. and Roghmann K.J., 'Prenatal care and pregnancy outcome in an HMO and general population: a multivariate cohort analysis', *American Journal of Public Health*, Vol. 71, 1984, pp. 381-90.

[111] Shiono P.H., Klebanoff M.A., Graubard B.I., Berendes H.W. and Rhoads G.G., 'Birth weight among women of different ethnic groups', *Journal of the American Medical Association*, Vol. 255, 1986, pp. 48-52.

[112] Shapiro S., Venet W., Strax P., Venet L., Roeser R., 'Ten- to fourteen-year effect of screening on breast cancer mortality', *Journal of the National Cancer Institute*, Vol. 69, 1982, pp. 349-55.

[113] Tabar L., Fagerberg C.J., Gad A. et al., 'Reduction in mortality from breast cancer after mass screening with mammography', *Lancet*, Vol. i, 1985, pp. 829-32.

[114] Lynge E., Madsen M. and Engholm G., 'Effect of organised screening on incidence

and mortality of cervical cancer in Denmark', *Cancer Research*, Vol. 49, 1989, pp. 2157-60.

[115] IARC Working Group on evaluation of cervical cancer screening programmes, 'Screening for squamous cell cancer: duration of low risk after negative results of cervical cytology and its implication for screening policies', *British Medical Journal*, Vol. 293, 1986, pp. 659-64.

[116] Stanley K., 'Control of tobacco production and use', in Jamieson D.T., Mosley W.H., Measham A.R. and Bobadilla J.L. (eds), *Disease control priorities in developing countries*, Oxford Medical Publications, Oxford, 1993.

[117] Leroy B., *The community of twelve and drug demand; comparative study of legislation and judicial practice,* Commission of the European Communities, Brussels, 1991.

[118] Farrell M., Strang J., Neeleman J., Reuter P., 'Policy on drug misuse in Europe', *British Medical Journal*, Vol. 308, 1994, pp. 609-10.

[119] Russell L.B., *Is Prevention Better than Cure?*, Brookings, Washington, 1986, p. 17.

[120] Axnick N.W. et al., 'Benefits due to immunisation against measles', *Public Health Reports*, Vol. 84, August 1969, pp. 673-80.

[121] Knox E.G., 'Strategy for Rubella Vaccination', *International Journal of Epidemiology*, Vol. 9, No. 1, 1980, pp. 13-23.

[122] Miller D.L. et al.,'Whooping cough and whooping cough vaccine: the risks and benefits debate', in Nathanson N. and Gordis L. (eds.), *Epidemiological Reviews*, Vol. 4, 1982, pp. 1-23.

[123] Russell L.B., op. cit. pp. 37-8.

[124] Office of Technology Assessment, *A Review of Selected Federal Vaccine and Immunization Policies*, Government Printing Office, Washington, 1979, chap. 4.

[125] *ibid.*, p. 31.

[126] Macleod-Clark J. et al., 'Helping patients and clients to stop smoking Phase 2: assessing the effectiveness of the nurses's role', *Research Report No. 19*, Health Education Authority, London 1987.

[127] *Effective Health Care*, No. 7, University of Leeds, November 1993.

[128] Pelletier K., 'A review and analysis of the health and cost-effectiveness outcome studies of comprehensive health promotion and disease prevention programs', *American Journal of Health Promotion*, Vol. 5, 1991, pp. 311-5.

[129] Fries J. F. et al., 'Reducing health care costs by reducing the need and demand for medical services', *New England Journal of Medicine*, Vol. 329, 1993, p. 321.

[130] Royal College of Physicians, *Report on Preventive Medicine*, London, 1991, p. 321.

[131] Russell L.B., op.cit., pp. 65-6.

[132] Teeling-Smith G., 'Economies of cardiovascular disease', in Sleight, P. (ed.), *Risk Factors and Coronary Heart Disease*, Mediq, London, 1988.

[133] Gellert G., 'International migration and control of communicable diseases',

Social Science and Medicine, Vol. 37, No. 12, 1993, pp. 1489-99.

[134] Davaki K., Mossialos E.,'Health Policies', in Kazakos P., Ioakimidis P.C., *Greece and the EC Membership Evaluated*, Pinter Publishers, London, 1994.

[135] Faculty of Public Health Medicine, *UK Levels of Health*, First Report, 1991, Second report, 1992 and Third report, 1993.

[136] Silman A.P., Allwright S.P.A., (ed), *The Elimination or Reduction of Disease? Opportunities for Health Service Action in Europe*, Oxford Medical Publications, 1988.

[137] Phelps C.E., 'Death and taxes: an opportunity for substitution', *Journal of Health Economics*, Vol. 7, 1988, pp. 1-24.

[138] Smith D.I., 'Impact in traffic safety of the introduction of Sunday alcohol sales in Perth, Western Australia', *Journal for the Studies of Alcohol*, Vol. 39, 1978, pp. 1302-4.

[139] Godfrey C., Maynard A., 'Economic aspects of tobacco use and taxation policy', *British Medical Journal*, Vol. 297, 1988, pp. 339-43.

[140] Greenberg G., 'MRC trial of treatment of mild hypertension: Principal results', *British Medical Journal*, Vol. 291, 1985, pp. 97-104.

[141] Multiple Risk Factor Intervention Trial Research Group, 'Multiple risk factor intervention trial. Risk factor changes and mortality results', *Journal of the American Medical Association*, Vol. 248, 1982, pp. 1465-77.

[142] Oliver M.F., Heady J.A., Morris J.N. et al., 'WHO cooperative trial on primary prevention of ischaemic heart disease using clofibrate to lower serum cholesterol: final mortality follow-up', *Lancet*, Vol. ii, 1984, pp. 600-4.

[143] Frick M.H., Elo O., Haapa K. et al., 'Helsinki heart study: primary prevention trial with gemfibrozil in middle-aged men with dyslipidaemia', *New England Journal of Medicine*, Vol. 317, 1987, pp. 1237-45.

[144] Department of Health, *Shaping a healthier future*, Stationery Office, Dublin, 1994.

Index

abdominal hernia 87, 88
Abril report 49–50
accidents *see* motor vehicle accidents
advertising, control of 108, 115, 134, 137,
139, 150, 151
AFAS 61
age
avoidable deaths by age range 88
cut-off, and burden of disease 87
distribution 1, 30, 58, 127
leading causes of death by age and sex 7
and motor vehicle accidents 12
see also elderly people
AIDS *see* HIV/AIDS
alcohol consumption 10
preventive interventions and health
promotion 101, 102, 107, 109–10, 114,
132, 134, 143, 145, 146, 147
taxation 109–10, 115, 136, 139, 151
Alma Ata declaration (1978) 131
ambulance services 43
ANDEM 60
antenatal care *see* maternal health
appendectomies 56
see also appendicitis
appendicitis 88, 89
see also appendectomies
armed forces 69
arthritis 141
asthma 9, 15, 88, 89, 90

asylum seekers 120, 122
Audit Commission 65
avoidable deaths 87–90, 131, 134, 146, 150

BCG immunization 103
Belgium
AIDS 16, 145
avoidable deaths 88, 89
breast cancer 13–14
cardiovascular disease 11
cerebrovascular disease 12
cervical cancer 13
cost containment 40–48 *passim*
expenditure on health care 29–32
government role 72–3, 74
inequalities in health and health service 20
infant mortality 4–6
life expectancy 2–3, 20
low weight births 6
lung cancer 8–9
maternal mortality 5
migrants and ethnic minorities 117, 118,
119, 145
ministerial responsibilities 68
organization and financing of health care
24, 26, 27
perinatal mortality 5–6
preventive interventions and health
promotion 74, 102–5 *passim*, 108–11
passim, 145

163